I0158544

# John Marr & Other Poems by Herman Melville

In 1847 Herman Melville married Elizabeth Shaw and after initially settling in New York they moved to Massachusetts. By 1851 his masterpiece, Moby Dick, was ready and published. It is perhaps, and certainly at the time, one of the most ambitious novels ever written. However it never sold out its initial print run of 3,000 and Melville's earnings on this masterpiece was $556.37.

In succeeding years his reputation waned and he found life increasingly difficult. His family was growing, now four children, and a stable income was essential. By 1855 with his writings almost ignored he joined the New York Customs house and worked there for the next 19 years.

He published his last book in 1857 to little notice. Despite periods of drinking, depression and other ails Elizabeth stood by her husband despite calls from other family members and the marriage held together.

In the 1860's he wrote many poems, many based on the Civil War. But there was no publisher for him and no audience. In 1876 he was at last able to publish privately his 16,000 line epic poem Clare! It was to no avail. By 1885 with his wife's inheritances they were able to retire.

Herman Melville, novelist, poet, short story writer and essayist, died at his home on September 28th 1891. He was the first writer to have his works collected and published by the Library of America. Here we publish his remarkable collection 'John Marr & Other Poems'.

## Index Of Poems

## JOHN MARR AND OTHER SAILORS

Since as in night's deck-watch ye show,
Why, lads, so silent here to me,
Your watchmate of times long ago?
Once, for all the darkling sea,
You your voices raised how clearly,
Striking in when tempest sung;
Hoisting up the storm-sail cheerly,
Life is storm, let storm! you rung.
Taking things as fated merely,
Childlike though the world ye spanned;
Nor holding unto life too dearly,
Ye who held your lives in hand
Skimmers, who on oceans four

Petrels were, and larks ashore.

O, not from memory lightly flung,
Forgot, like strains no more availing,
The heart to music haughtier strung;
Nay, frequent near me, never staleing,
Whose good feeling kept ye young.
Like tides that enter creek or stream,
Ye come, ye visit me, or seem
Swimming out from seas of faces,
Alien myriads memory traces,
To enfold me in a dream!

I yearn as ye. But rafts that strain,
Parted, shall they lock again?
Twined we were, entwined, then riven,
Ever to new embracements driven,
Shifting gulf-weed of the main!
And how if one here shift no more,
Lodged by the flinging surge ashore?
Nor less, as now, in eve's decline,
Your shadowy fellowship is mine.
Ye float around me, form and feature:
Tattooings, ear-rings, love-locks curled;
Barbarians of man's simpler nature,
Unworldly servers of the world.
Yea, present all, and dear to me,
Though shades, or scouring China's sea.

Whither, whither, merchant-sailors,
Whitherward now in roaring gales?
Competing still, ye huntsman-whalers,
In leviathan's wake what boat prevails?
And man-of-war's men, whereaway?
If now no dinned drum beat to quarters
On the wilds of midnight waters
Foemen looming through the spray;
Do yet your gangway lanterns, streaming,
Vainly strive to pierce below,
When, tilted from the slant plank gleaming,
A brother you see to darkness go?

But, gunmates lashed in shotted canvas,
If where long watch-below ye keep,
Never the shrill "All hands up hammocks!"
Breaks the spell that charms your sleep,
And summoning trumps might vainly call,

And booming guns implore
A beat, a heart-beat musters all,
One heart-beat at heart-core.
It musters. But to clasp, retain;
To see you at the halyards main
To hear your chorus once again!


## BRIDEGROOM DICK
1876

Sunning ourselves in October on a day
Balmy as spring, though the year was in decay,
I lading my pipe, she stirring her tea,
My old woman she says to me,
"Feel ye, old man, how the season mellows?"
And why should I not, blessed heart alive,
Here mellowing myself, past sixty-five,
To think o' the May-time o' pennoned young
fellows
This stripped old hulk here for years may
survive.

Ere yet, long ago, we were spliced, Bonny Blue,
(Silvery it gleams down the moon-glade o' time,
Ah, sugar in the bowl and berries in the prime!)
Coxswain I o' the Commodore's crew,
Under me the fellows that manned his fine gig,
Spinning him ashore, a king in full fig.
Chirrupy even when crosses rubbed me,
Bridegroom Dick lieutenants dubbed me.
Pleasant at a yarn, Bob o' Linkum in a song,
Diligent in duty and nattily arrayed,
Favored I was, wife, and fleeted right along;
And though but a tot for such a tall grade,
A high quartermaster at last I was made.

All this, old lassie, you have heard before,
But you listen again for the sake e'en o' me;
No babble stales o' the good times o' yore
To Joan, if Darby the babbler be.

Babbler? O' what? Addled brains, they
forget!
O quartermaster I; yes, the signals set,
Hoisted the ensign, mended it when frayed,
Polished up the binnacle, minded the helm,

And prompt every order blithely obeyed.
To me would the officers say a word cheery
Break through the starch o' the quarter-deck
realm;
His coxswain late, so the Commodore's pet.
Ay, and in night-watches long and weary,
Bored nigh to death with the navy etiquette,
Yearning, too, for fun, some younker, a cadet,
Dropping for time each vain bumptious trick,
Boy-like would unbend to Bridegroom Dick.
But a limit there was, a check, d' ye see:
Those fine young aristocrats knew their degree.

Well, stationed aft where their lordships
keep,
Seldom going forward excepting to sleep,
I, boozing now on by-gone years,
My betters recall along with my peers.
Recall them? Wife, but I see them plain:
Alive, alert, every man stirs again.
Ay, and again on the lee-side pacing,
My spy-glass carrying, a truncheon in show,
Turning at the taffrail, my footsteps retracing,
Proud in my duty, again methinks I go.
And Dave, Dainty Dave, I mark where he
stands,
Our trim sailing-master, to time the high-noon,
That thingumbob sextant perplexing eyes and
hands,
Squinting at the sun, or twigging o' the moon;
Then, touching his cap to Old Chock-a-Block
Commanding the quarter-deck, "Sir, twelve
o'clock."

Where sails he now, that trim sailing-master,
Slender, yes, as the ship's sky-s'l pole?
Dimly I mind me of some sad disaster
Dainty Dave was dropped from the navy-roll!
And ah, for old Lieutenant Chock-a-Block
Fast, wife, chock-fast to death's black dock!
Buffeted about the obstreperous ocean,
Fleeted his life, if lagged his promotion.
Little girl, they are all, all gone, I think,
Leaving Bridegroom Dick here with lids that
wink.

Where is Ap Catesby? The fights fought of

yore
Famed him, and laced him with epaulets, and
more.
But fame is a wake that after-wakes cross,
And the waters wallow all, and laugh
Where's the loss?
But John Bull's bullet in his shoulder bearing
Ballasted Ap in his long sea-faring.
The middies they ducked to the man who had
messed
With Decatur in the gun-room, or forward
pressed
Fighting beside Perry, Hull, Porter, and the
rest.

Humped veteran o' the Heart-o'-Oak war,
Moored long in haven where the old heroes are,
Never on you did the iron-clads jar!
Your open deck when the boarder assailed,
The frank old heroic hand-to-hand then availed.

But where's Guert Gan? Still heads he the van?
As before Vera-Cruz, when he dashed splashing
through
The blue rollers sunned, in his brave gold-and-
blue,
And, ere his cutter in keel took the strand,
Aloft waved his sword on the hostile land!
Went up the cheering, the quick chanticleering;
All hands vying, all colors flying:
"Cock-a-doodle-doo!" and "Row, boys, row!"
"Hey, Starry Banner!" "Hi, Santa Anna!"
Old Scott's young dash at Mexico.

Fine forces o' the land, fine forces o' the sea,
Fleet, army, and flotilla, tell, heart o' me,
Tell, if you can, whereaway now they be!

But ah, how to speak of the hurricane
Unchained
The Union's strands parted in the hawser
over-strained;
Our flag blown to shreds, anchors gone
Altogether
The dashed fleet o' States in Secession's foul
weather.

Lost in the smother o' that wide public stress,
In hearts, private hearts, what ties there were
snapped!
Tell, Hal, vouch, Will, o' the ward-room mess,
On you how the riving thunder-bolt clapped.
With a bead in your eye and beads in your glass,
And a grip o' the flipper, it was part and pass:
"Hal, must it be: Well, if come indeed the
shock,
To North or to South, let the victory cleave,
Vaunt it he may on his dung-hill the cock,
But Uncle Sam's eagle never crow will,
believe."

Sentiment: ay, while suspended hung all,
Ere the guns against Sumter opened there
the ball,
And partners were taken, and the red dance
began,
War's red dance o' death! Well, we, to a man,
We sailors o' the North, wife, how could we
lag?
Strike with your kin, and you stick to the flag!
But to sailors o' the South that easy way was
barred.
To some, dame, believe (and I speak o' what I
know),
Wormwood the trial and the Uzzite's black
shard;
And the faithfuller the heart, the crueller the
throe.
Duty? It pulled with more than one string,
This way and that, and anyhow a sting.
The flag and your kin, how be true unto both?
If either plight ye keep, then ye break the other
troth.
But elect here they must, though the casuists
were out;
Decide, hurry up, and throttle every doubt.

Of all these thrills thrilled at keelson, and
throes,
Little felt the shoddyites a-toasting o' their
toes;
In mart and bazar Lucre chuckled the huzza,
Coining the dollars in the bloody mint of war.

But in men, gray knights o' the Order o' Scars,
And brave boys bound by vows unto Mars,
Nature grappled honor, intertwisting in the
strife:
But some cut the knot with a thoroughgoing
knife.
For how when the drums beat? How in the fray
In Hampton Roads on the fine balmy day?

There a lull, wife, befell, drop o' silent in the
din.
Let us enter that silence ere the belchings
re-begin.
Through a ragged rift aslant in the cannonade's
smoke
An iron-clad reveals her repellent broadside
Bodily intact. But a frigate, all oak,
Shows honeycombed by shot, and her deck
crimson-dyed.
And a trumpet from port of the iron-clad hails,
Summoning the other, whose flag never trails:
"Surrender that frigate, Will! Surrender,
Or I will sink her, ram, and end her!"

'T was Hal. And Will, from the naked heart-o'-oak,
Will, the old messmate, minus trumpet, spoke,
Informally intrepid, "Sink her, and be
damned!"
Enough. Gathering way, the iron-clad rammed.
The frigate, heeling over, on the wave threw a
dusk.
Not sharing in the slant, the clapper of her bell
The fixed metal struck, uinvoked struck the
knell
Of the Cumberland stillettoed by the
Merrimac's tusk;
While, broken in the wound underneath the
gun-deck,
Like a sword-fish's blade in leviathan waylaid,
The tusk was left infixed in the fast-foundering
wreck.
There, dungeoned in the cockpit, the wounded
go down,
And the chaplain with them. But the surges
uplift
The prone dead from deck, and for moment
they drift

Washed with the swimmers, and the spent
swimmers drown.
Nine fathom did she sink, erect, though hid
from light
Save her colors unsurrendered and spars that
kept the height.

Nay, pardon, old aunty! Wife, never let it fall,
That big started tear that hovers on the brim;
I forgot about your nephew and the Merrimac's
ball;
No more then of her, since it summons up him.
But talk o' fellows' hearts in the wine's genial
cup:
Trap them in the fate, jam them in the strait,
Guns speak their hearts then, and speak
right up.
The troublous colic o' intestine war
It sets the bowels o' affection ajar.
But, lord, old dame, so spins the whizzing world,
A humming-top, ay, for the little boy-gods
Flogging it well with their smart little rods,
Tittering at time and the coil uncurled.

Now, now, sweetheart, you sidle away,
No, never you like that kind o' gay;
But sour if I get, giving truth her due,
Honey-sweet forever, wife, will Dick be to you!

But avast with the War! 'Why recall racking
days
Since set up anew are the slip's started stays?
Nor less, though the gale we have left behind,
Well may the heave o' the sea remind.
It irks me now, as it troubled me then,
To think o' the fate in the madness o' men.
If Dick was with Farragut on the night-river,
When the boom-chain we burst in the fire-raft's
glare,
That blood-dyed the visage as red as the liver;
In the Battle for the Bay too if Dick had a
share,
And saw one aloft a-piloting the war
Trumpet in the whirlwind, a Providence in
place
Our Admiral old whom the captains huzza,
Dick joys in the man nor brags about the race.

But better, wife, I like to booze on the days
Ere the Old Order foundered in these very
frays,
And tradition was lost and we learned strange
ways.
Often I think on the brave cruises then;
Re-sailing them in memory, I hail the press o'
men
On the gunned promenade where rolling they
go,
Ere the dog-watch expire and break up the
show.
The Laced Caps I see between forward guns;
Away from the powder-room they puff the
cigar;
"Three days more, hey, the donnas and the
dons!"
"Your Zeres widow, will you hunt her up,
Starr?"
The Laced Caps laugh, and the bright waves
too;
Very jolly, very wicked, both sea and crew,
Nor heaven looks sour on either, I guess,
Nor Pecksniff he bosses the gods' high mess.
Wistful ye peer, wife, concerned for my head,
And how best to get me betimes to my bed.

But king o' the club, the gayest golden spark,
Sailor o' sailors, what sailor do I mark?
Tom Tight, Tom Tight, no fine fellow finer,
A cutwater nose, ay, a spirited soul;
But, bowsing away at the well-brewed bowl,
He never bowled back from that last voyage to
China.

Tom was lieutenant in the brig-o'-war famed
When an officer was hung for an arch-mutineer,
But a mystery cleaved, and the captain was
blamed,
And a rumpus too raised, though his honor
it was clear.
And Tom he would say, when the mousers
would try him,
And with cup after cup o' Burgundy ply him:
"Gentlemen, in vain with your wassail you
beset,

For the more I tipple, the tighter do I get."
No blabber, no, not even with the can
True to himself and loyal to his clan.

Tom blessed us starboard and damned us larboard,
Right down from rail to the streak o' the
garboard.
Nor less, wife, we liked him. Tom was a man
In contrast queer with Chaplain Le Fan,
Who blessed us at morn, and at night yet again,
Damning us only in decorous strain;
Preaching 'tween the guns, each cutlass in its
Place
From text that averred old Adam a hard case.
I see him, Tom, on horse-block standing,
Trumpet at mouth, thrown up all amain,
An elephant's bugle, vociferous demanding
Of topmen aloft in the hurricane of rain,
"Letting that sail there your faces flog?
Manhandle it, men, and you'll get the good
grog!"
O Tom, but he knew a blue-jacket's ways,
And how a lieutenant may genially haze;
Only a sailor sailors heartily praise.

Wife, where be all these chaps, I wonder?
Trumpets in the tempest, terrors in the fray,
Boomed their commands along the deck like
thunder;
But silent is the sod, and thunder dies away.
But Captain Turret, "Old Hemlock" tall,
(A leaning tower when his tank brimmed all,)
Manoeuvre out alive from the war did he?
Or, too old for that, drift under the lee?
Kentuckian colossal, who, touching at Madeira,
The huge puncheon shipped o' prime
Santa-Clara;
Then rocked along the deck so solemnly!
No whit the less though judicious was enough
In dealing with the Finn who made the great
huff;
Our three-decker's giant, a grand boatswain's
mate,
Manliest of men in his own natural senses;
But driven stark mad by the devil's drugged
stuff,
Storming all aboard from his run-ashore late,

Challenging to battle, vouchsafing no pretenses,
A reeling King Ogg, delirious in power,
The quarter-deck carronades he seemed to
make cower.
"Put him in brig there!" said Lieutenant
Marrot.
"Put him in brig!" back he mocked like a
parrot;
"Try it, then!" swaying a fist like Thor's
sledge,
And making the pigmy constables hedge
Ship's corporals and the master-at-arms.
"In brig there, I say!" They dally no more;
Like hounds let slip on a desperate boar,
Together they pounce on the formidable Finn,
Pinion and cripple and hustle him in.
Anon, under sentry, between twin guns,
He slides off in drowse, and the long night runs.

Morning brings a summons. Whistling it calls,
Shrilled through the pipes of the boatswain's
four aids;
Trilled down the hatchways along the dusk
halls:
Muster to the Scourge! Dawn of doom and
its blast!
As from cemeteries raised, sailors swarm before
the mast,
Tumbling up the ladders from the ship's nether
shades.

Keeping in the background and taking small
part,
Lounging at their ease, indifferent in face,
Behold the trim marines uncompromised in
heart;
Their Major, buttoned up, near the staff finds
Room
The staff o' lieutenants standing grouped in
their place.
All the Laced Caps o' the ward-room come,
The Chaplain among them, disciplined and
dumb.
The blue-nosed boatswain, complexioned like
slag,
Like a blue Monday lours, his implements in
bag.

Executioners, his aids, a couple by him stand,
At a nod there the thongs to receive from his hand.
Never venturing a caveat whatever may betide,
Though functionally here on humanity's side,
The grave Surgeon shows, like the formal
physician
Attending the rack o' the Spanish Inquisition.

The angel o' the "brig" brings his prisoner up;
Then, steadied by his old Santa-Clara, a sup,
Heading all erect, the ranged assizes there,
Lo, Captain Turret, and under starred
bunting,
(A florid full face and fine silvered hair,)
Gigantic the yet greater giant confronting.

Now the culprit he liked, as a tall captain can
A Titan subordinate and true sailor-man;
And frequent he'd shown it, no worded
advance,
But flattering the Finn with a well-timed glance.
But what of that now? In the martinet-mien
Read the Articles of War, heed the naval
routine;
While, cut to the heart a dishonor there to win,
Restored to his senses, stood the Anak Finn;
In racked self-control the squeezed tears
peeping,
Scalding the eye with repressed inkeeping.
Discipline must be; the scourge is deemed due.
But ah for the sickening and strange heart-
benumbing,
Compassionate abasement in shipmates that view;
Such a grand champion shamed there succumbing!
"Brown, tie him up." The cord he brooked:
How else? his arms spread apart, never
threaping;
No, never he flinched, never sideways he looked,
Peeled to the waistband, the marble flesh
creeping,
Lashed by the sleet the officious winds urge.

In function his fellows their fellowship merge
The twain standing nigh, the two boatswain's
mates,
Sailors of his grade, ay, and brothers of his
mess.

With sharp thongs adroop the junior one
awaits
The word to uplift.
"Untie him so!
Submission is enough, Man, you may go."
Then, promenading aft, brushing fat Purser
Smart,
"Flog? Never meant it, hadn't any heart.
Degrade that tall fellow? "Such, wife, was he,
Old Captain Turret, who the brave wine could
stow.
Magnanimous, you think? But what does
Dick see?
Apron to your eye! Why, never fell a blow;
Cheer up, old wifie, 't was a long time ago.

But where's that sore one, crabbed and-severe,
Lieutenant Lon Lumbago, an arch scrutineer?
Call the roll to-day, would he answer. Here!
When the Blixum's fellows to quarters
mustered
How he'd lurch along the lane of gun-crews
clustered,
Testy as touchwood, to pry and to peer.
Jerking his sword underneath larboard arm,
He ground his worn grinders to keep himself
calm.
Composed in his nerves, from the fidgets set
free,
Tell, Sweet Wrinkles, alive now is he,
In Paradise a parlor where the even
tempers be?

Where's Commander All-a-Tanto?
Where's Orlop Bob singing up from below?
Where's Rhyming Ned? has he spun his last
canto?
Where's Jewsharp Jim? Where's Ringadoon
Joe?
Ah, for the music over and done,
The band all dismissed save the droned
trombone!
Where's Glenn o' the gun-room, who loved
Hot-Scotch
Glen, prompt and cool in a perilous watch?
Where's flaxen-haired Phil? a gray lieutenant?
Or rubicund, flying a dignified pennant?

But where sleeps his brother? the cruise it was
o'er,
But ah, for death's grip that welcomed him
ashore!
Where's Sid, the cadet, so frank in his brag,
Whose toast was audacious "Here's Sid, and
Sid's flag!"
Like holiday-craft that have sunk unknown,
May a lark of a lad go lonely down?
Who takes the census under the sea?
Can others like old ensigns be,
Bunting I hoisted to flutter at the gaff
Rags in end that once were flags
Gallant streaming from the staff?

Such scurvy doom could the chances deal
To Top-Gallant Harry and Jack Genteel?
Lo, Genteel Jack in hurricane weather,
Shagged like a bear, like a red lion roaring;
But O, so fine in his chapeau and feather,
In port to the ladies never once jawing;
All bland politesse, how urbane was he
"Oui, mademoiselle", "Ma chère amie!"

'T was Jack got up the ball at Naples,
Gay in the old Ohio glorious;
His hair was curled by the berth-deck barber,
Never you'd deemed him a cub of rude Boreas;
In tight little pumps, with the grand dames in
rout,
A-flinging his shapely foot all about;
His watch-chain with love's jeweled tokens
abounding,
Curls ambrosial shaking out odors,
Waltzing along the batteries, astounding
The gunner glum and the grim-visaged loaders.

Wife, where be all these blades, I wonder,
Pennoned fine fellows, so strong, so gay?
Never their colors with a dip dived under;
Have they hauled them down in a lack-lustre
day,
Or beached their boats in the Far, Far Away?
Hither and thither, blown wide asunder,
Where's this fleet, I wonder and wonder.
Slipt their cables, rattled their adieu,

(Whereaway pointing? to what rendezvous?)
Out of sight, out of mind, like the crack
Constitution,
And many a keel time never shall renew
Bon Homme Dick o' the buff Revolution,
The Black Cockade and the staunch True-Blue.

Doff hats to Decatur! But where is his blazon?
Must merited fame endure time's wrong
Glory's ripe grape wizen up to a raisin?
Yes! for Nature teems, and the years are
strong,
And who can keep the tally o' the names that
fleet along!

But his frigate, wife, his bride? Would
blacksmiths brown
Into smithereens smite the solid old renown?
Rivetting the bolts in the iron-clad's shell,
Hark to the hammers with a rat-tat-tat;
"Handier a derby than a laced cocked hat!
The Monitor was ugly, but she served us right
well,
Better than the Cumberland, a beauty and the
belle."

Better than the Cumberland! Heart alive
in me!
That battlemented hull, Tantallon o' the sea,
Kicked in, as at Boston the taxed chests o' tea!
Ay, spurned by the ram, once a tall, shapely
craft,
But lopped by the Rebs to an iron-beaked
Raft
A blacksmith's unicorn in armor cap-a-pie.

Under the water-line a ram's blow is dealt:
And foul fall the knuckles that strike below the
belt.
Nor brave the inventions that serve to replace
The openness of valor while dismantling the
grace.

Aloof from all this and the never-ending game,
Tantamount to teetering, plot and counterplot;
Impenetrable armor, all-perforating shot;
Aloof, bless God, ride the war-ships of old,

A grand fleet moored in the roadstead of fame;
Not submarine sneaks with them are enrolled;
Their long shadows dwarf us, their flags are as
flame.

Don't fidget so, wife; an old man's passion
Amounts to no more than this smoke that I
puff;
There, there, now, buss me in good old fashion;
A died-down candle will flicker in the snuff.

But one last thing let your old babbler say,
What Decatur's coxswain said who was long
ago hearsed,
"Take in your flying-kites, for there comes a
lubber's day
When gallant things will go, and the three-
deckers first."

My pipe is smoked out, and the grog runs
slack;
But bowse away, wife, at your blessed Bohea;
This empty can here must needs solace me
Nay, sweetheart, nay; I take that back;
Dick drinks from your eyes and he finds no
lack!


## TOM DEADLIGHT

During a tempest encountered homeward-bound from the Mediterranean,
a grizzled petty-officer, one of the two captains of the forecastle, dying at
night in his hammock, swung in the sick-bay under the tiered gun-decks
of the British Dreadnaught, 98, wandering in his mind, though with
glimpses of sanity, and starting up at whiles, sings by snatches his good-
bye and last injunctions to two messmates, his watchers, one of whom
fans the fevered tar with the flap of his old sou'wester. Some names and
phrases, with here and there a line, or part of one; these, in his
aberration, wrested into incoherency from their original connection and
import, he voluntarily derives, as he does the measure, from a famous old
sea-ditty, whose cadences, long rife, and now humming in the collapsing
brain, attune the last flutterings of distempered thought.

Farewell and adieu to you noble hearties,
Farewell and adieu to you ladies of Spain,
For I've received orders for to sail for the
Deadman,

But hope with the grand fleet to see you
again.

I have hove my ship to, with main-top-sail
aback, boys;
I have hove my ship to, for the strike
soundings clear
The black scud a'flying; but, by God's blessing,
dam' me,
Right up the Channel for the Deadman I'll
steer.

I have worried through the waters that are
called the Doldrums,
And growled at Sargasso that clogs while ye
Grope
Blast my eyes, but the light-ship is hid by the
mist, lads:
Flying Dutchman, odds bobbs, off the
Cape of Good Hope!

But what's this I feel that is fanning my cheek,
Matt?
The white goney's wing? how she rolls!
't is the Cape!
Give my kit to the mess, Jock, for kin none is
mine, none;
And tell Holy Joe to avast with the crape.

Dead reckoning, says Joe, it won't do to go by;
But they doused all the glims, Matt, in sky
t' other night.
Dead reckoning is good for to sail for the
Deadman;
And Tom Deadlight he thinks it may reckon
near right.

The signal! it streams for the grand fleet to
anchor.
The captains, the trumpets, the hullabaloo!
Stand by for blue-blazes, and mind your
shank-painters,
For the Lord High Admiral, he's squinting
at you!

But give me my tot, Matt, before I roll over;
Jock, let's have your flipper, it's good for to

feel;
And don't sew me up without baccy in mouth,
boys,
And don't blubber like lubbers when I turn
up my keel.


## JACK ROY

Kept up by relays of generations young
Never dies at halyards the blithe chorus sung;
While in sands, sounds, and seas where the
storm-petrels cry,
Dropped mute around the globe, these halyard
singers lie.
Short-lived the clippers for racing-cups that
run,
And speeds in life's career many a lavish
mother's-son.

But thou, manly king o' the old Splendid's
crew,
The ribbons o' thy hat still a-fluttering, should
Fly
A challenge, and forever, nor the bravery
should rue.
Only in a tussle for the starry flag high,
When 'tis piety to do, and privilege to die.
Then, only then, would heaven think to lop
Such a cedar as the captain o' the Splendid's
main-top:
A belted sea-gentleman; a gallant, off-hand
Mercutio indifferent in life's gay command.
Magnanimous in humor; when the splintering
shot fell,
"Tooth-picks a-plenty, lads; thank 'em with a
shell!"

Sang Larry o' the Cannakin, smuggler o' the
wine,
At mess between guns, lad in jovial recline:
"In Limbo our Jack he would chirrup up a
cheer,
The martinet there find a chaffing mutineer;
From a thousand fathoms down under hatches
o' your Hades,
He'd ascend in love-ditty, kissing fingers to

your ladies!"

Never relishing the knave, though allowing
for the menial,
Nor overmuch the king, Jack, nor prodigally
genial.
Ashore on liberty he flashed in escapade,
Vaulting over life in its levelness of grade,
Like the dolphin off Africa in rainbow
a-sweeping
Arch iridescent shot from seas languid
sleeping.

Larking with thy life, if a joy but a toy,
Heroic in thy levity wert thou, Jack Roy.


## Sea Pieces

### THE HAGLETS

By chapel bare, with walls sea-beat
The lichened urns in wilds are lost
About a carved memorial stone
That shows, decayed and coral-mossed,
A form recumbent, swords at feet,
Trophies at head, and kelp for a
winding-sheet.

I invoke thy ghost, neglected fane,
Washed by the waters' long lament;
I adjure the recumbent effigy
To tell the cenotaph's intent
Reveal why fagotted swords are at feet,
Why trophies appear and weeds are the
winding-sheet.

By open ports the Admiral sits,
And shares repose with guns that tell
Of power that smote the arm'd Plate Fleet
Whose sinking flag-ship's colors fell;
But over the Admiral floats in light
His squadron's flag, the red-cross Flag
of the White.

The eddying waters whirl astern,

The prow, a seedsman, sows the spray;
With bellying sails and buckling spars
The black hull leaves a Milky Way;
Her timbers thrill, her batteries roll,
She revelling speeds exulting with pennon
at pole,

But ah, for standards captive trailed
For all their scutcheoned castles' pride
Castilian towers that dominate Spain,
Naples, and either Ind beside;
Those haughty towers, armorial ones,
Rue the salute from the Admiral's dens
of guns.

Ensigns and arms in trophy brave,
Braver for many a rent and scar,
The captor's naval hall bedeck,
Spoil that insures an earldom's star
Toledoes great, grand draperies, too,
Spain's steel and silk, and splendors from
Peru.

But crippled part in splintering fight,
The vanquished flying the victor's flags,
With prize-crews, under convoy-guns,
Heavy the fleet from Opher drags
The Admiral crowding sail ahead,
Foremost with news who foremost in conflict
sped.

But out from cloistral gallery dim,
In early night his glance is thrown;
He marks the vague reserve of heaven,
He feels the touch of ocean lone;
Then turns, in frame part undermined,
Nor notes the shadowing wings that fan
behind.

There, peaked and gray, three haglets fly,
And follow, follow fast in wake
Where slides the cabin-lustre shy,
And sharks from man a glamour take,
Seething along the line of light
In lane that endless rules the war-ship's flight.

The sea-fowl here, whose hearts none know,

They followed late the flag-ship quelled,
(As now the victor one) and long
Above her gurgling grave, shrill held
With screams their wheeling rites, then sped
Direct in silence where the victor led.

Now winds less fleet, but fairer, blow,
A ripple laps the coppered side,
While phosphor sparks make ocean gleam,
Like camps lit up in triumph wide;
With lights and tinkling cymbals meet
Acclaiming seas the advancing conqueror
greet.

But who a flattering tide may trust,
Or favoring breeze, or aught in end?
Careening under startling blasts
The sheeted towers of sails impend;
While, gathering bale, behind is bred
A livid storm-bow, like a rainbow dead.

At trumpet-call the topmen spring;
And, urged by after-call in stress,
Yet other tribes of tars ascend
The rigging's howling wilderness;
But ere yard-ends alert they win,
Hell rules in heaven with hurricane-fire
and din.

The spars, athwart at spiry height,
Like quaking Lima's crosses rock;
Like bees the clustering sailors cling
Against the shrouds, or take the shock
Flat on the swept yard-arms aslant,
Dipped like the wheeling condor's pinions
gaunt.

A LULL! and tongues of languid flame
Lick every boom, and lambent show
Electric 'gainst each face aloft;
The herds of clouds with bellowings go:
The black ship rears, beset, harassed,
Then plunges far with luminous antlers vast.

In trim betimes they turn from land,
Some shivered sails and spars they stow;
One watch, dismissed, they troll the can,

While loud the billow thumps the bow
Vies with the fist that smites the board,
Obstreperous at each reveller's jovial word.

Of royal oak by storms confirmed,
The tested hull her lineage shows:
Vainly the plungings whelm her prow
She rallies, rears, she sturdier grows:
Each shot-hole plugged, each storm-sail home,
With batteries housed she rams the watery
dome.

DIM seen adrift through driving scud,
The wan moon shows in plight forlorn;
Then, pinched in visage, fades and fades
Like to the faces drowned at morn,
When deeps engulfed the flag-ship's crew,
And, shrilling round, the inscrutable haglets
flew.

And still they fly, nor now they cry,
But constant fan a second wake,
Unflagging pinions ply and ply,
Abreast their course intent they take;
Their silence marks a stable mood,
They patient keep their eager neighborhood.

Plumed with a smoke, a confluent sea,
Heaved in a combing pyramid full,
Spent at its climax, in collapse
Down headlong thundering stuns the hull:
The trophy drops; but, reared again,
Shows Mars' high-altar and contemns the
main.

REBUILT it stands, the brag of arms,
Transferred in site, no thought of where
The sensitive needle keeps its place,
And starts, disturbed, a quiverer there;
The helmsman rubs the clouded glass
Peers in, but lets the trembling portent pass.

Let pass as well his shipmates do
(Whose dream of power no tremors jar)
Fears for the fleet convoyed astern:
"Our flag they fly, they share our star;
Spain's galleons great in hull are stout:

Manned by our men, like us they'll ride it
out."

Tonight's the night that ends the week
Ends day and week and month and year:
A fourfold imminent flickering time,
For now the midnight draws anear:
Eight bells! and passing-bells they be
The Old year fades, the Old Year dies at sea.

He launched them well. But shall the New
Redeem the pledge the Old Year made,
Or prove a self-asserting heir?
But healthy hearts few qualms invade:
By shot-chests grouped in bays 'tween guns
The gossips chat, the grizzled, sea-beat ones.

And boyish dreams some graybeards blab:
"To sea, my lads, we go no more
Who share the Acapulco prize;
We'll all night in, and bang the door;
Our ingots red shall yield us bliss:
Lads, golden years begin to-night with this!"

Released from deck, yet waiting call,
Glazed caps and coats baptized in storm,
A watch of Laced Sleeves round the board
Draw near in heart to keep them warm:
"Sweethearts and wives!" clink, clink, they
meet,
And, quaffing, dip in wine their beards of
sleet.
"Ay, let the star-light stay withdrawn,
So here her hearth-light memory fling,
So in this wine-light cheer be born,
And honor's fellowship weld our ring
Honor! our Admiral's aim foretold:

A tomb or a trophy, and lo, 't is a trophy and
gold!"
But he, a unit, sole in rank,
Apart needs keep his lonely state,
The sentry at his guarded door
Mute as by vault the sculptured Fate;
Belted he sits in drowsy light,
And, hatted, nods, the Admiral of the White.

He dozes, aged with watches passed
Years, years of pacing to and fro;
He dozes, nor attends the stir
In bullioned standards rustling low,
Nor minds the blades whose secret thrill
Perverts overhead the magnet's Polar will:

LESS heeds the shadowing three that play
And follow, follow fast in wake,
Untiring wing and lidless eye
Abreast their course intent they take;
Or sigh or sing, they hold for good
The unvarying flight and fixed inveterate
mood.

In dream at last his dozings merge,
In dream he reaps his victor's fruit;
The Flags-o'-the-Blue, the Flags-o'-the-Red,
Dipped flags of his country's fleets salute
His Flag-o'-the-White in harbor proud
But why should it blench? Why turn to a
painted shroud?

The hungry seas they hound the hull,
The sharks they dog the haglets' flight;
With one consent the winds, the waves
In hunt with fins and wings unite,
While drear the harps in cordage sound
Remindful wails for old Armadas drowned.

Ha, yonder! are they Northern Lights?
Or signals flashed to warn or ward?
Yea, signals lanced in breakers high;
But doom on warning follows hard:
While yet they veer in hope to shun,
They strike! and thumps of hull and heart are
one.

But beating hearts a drum-beat calls
And prompt the men to quarters go;
Discipline, curbing nature, rules
Heroic makes who duty know:
They execute the trump's command,
Or in peremptory places wait and stand.

Yet cast about in blind amaze
As through their watery shroud they peer:

"We tacked from land: then how betrayed?
Have currents swerved us, snared us here?"
None heed the blades that clash in place
Under lamps dashed down that lit the
magnet's case.

Ah, what may live, who mighty swim,
Or boat-crew reach that shore forbid,
Or cable span? Must victors drown
Perish, even as the vanquished did?
Man keeps from man the stifled moan;
They shouldering stand, yet each in heart
how lone.

Some heaven invoke; but rings of reefs
Prayer and despair alike deride
In dance of breakers forked or peaked,
Pale maniacs of the maddened tide;
While, strenuous yet some end to earn,
The haglets spin, though now no more astern.

Like shuttles hurrying in the looms
Aloft through rigging frayed they ply
Cross and recross, weave and inweave,
Then lock the web with clinching cry
Over the seas on seas that clasp
The weltering wreck where gurgling ends the
gasp.

Ah, for the Plate-Fleet trophy now,
The victor's voucher, flags and arms;
Never they'll hang in Abbey old
And take Time's dust with holier palms;
Nor less content, in liquid night,
Their captor sleeps, the Admiral of the
White.

Imbedded deep with shells
And drifted treasure deep,
Forever he sinks deeper in
Unfathomable sleep
His cannon round him thrown,
His sailors at his feet,
The wizard sea enchanting them
Where never haglets beat.

On nights when meteors play

And light the breakers dance,
The Oreads from the caves
With silvery elves advance;
And up from ocean stream,
And down from heaven far,
The rays that blend in dream
The abysm and the star.


## THE AEOLIAN HARP
At The Surf Inn

List the harp in window wailing
Stirred by fitful gales from sea:
Shrieking up in mad crescendo
Dying down in plaintive key!

Listen: less a strain ideal
Than Ariel's rendering of the Real.
What that Real is, let hint
A picture stamped in memory's mint.

Braced well up, with beams aslant,
Betwixt the continents sails the Phocion,
For Baltimore bound from Alicant.
Blue breezy skies white fleeces fleck
Over the chill blue white-capped ocean:
From yard-arm comes "Wreck ho, a
wreck!"

Dismasted and adrift,
Longtime a thing forsaken;
Overwashed by every wave
Like the slumbering kraken;
Heedless if the billow roar,
Oblivious of the lull,
Leagues and leagues from shoal or shore,
It swims, a levelled hull:
Bulwarks gone, a shaven wreck,
Nameless and a grass-green deck.
A lumberman: perchance, in hold
Prostrate pines with hemlocks rolled.

It has drifted, waterlogged,
Till by trailing weeds beclogged:
Drifted, drifted, day by day,
Pilotless on pathless way.

It has drifted till each plank
Is oozy as the oyster-bank:
Drifted, drifted, night by night,
Craft that never shows a light;
Nor ever, to prevent worse knell,
Tolls in fog the warning bell.

From collision never shrinking,
Drive what may through darksome smother;
Saturate, but never sinking,
Fatal only to the other!
Deadlier than the sunken reef
Since still the snare it shifteth,
Torpid in dumb ambuscade
Waylayingly it drifteth.

O, the sailors, O, the sails!
O, the lost crews never heard of!
Well the harp of Ariel wails
Thought that tongue can tell no word of!

## TO THE MASTER OF THE METEOR

Lonesome on earth's loneliest deep,
Sailor! who dost thy vigil keep
Off the Cape of Storms dost musing sweep
Over monstrous waves that curl and comb;
Of thee we think when here from brink
We blow the mead in bubbling foam.

Of thee we think, in a ring we link;
To the shearer of ocean's fleece we drink,
And the Meteor rolling home.

## FAR OFF-SHORE

Look, the raft, a signal flying,
Thin, a shred;
None upon the lashed spars lying,
Quick or dead.

Cries the sea-fowl, hovering over,
"Crew, the crew?"
And the billow, reckless, rover,
Sweeps anew!

## THE MAN-OF-WAR HAWK

Yon black man-of-war-hawk that wheels in
the light
O'er the black ship's white sky-s'l, sunned
cloud to the sight,
Have we low-flyers wings to ascend to his
height?
No arrow can reach him; nor thought can
attain
To the placid supreme in the sweep of his
reign.


## THE FIGURE-HEAD

The Charles-and-Emma seaward sped,
(Named from the carven pair at prow,)
He so smart, and a curly head,
She tricked forth as a bride knows how:
Pretty stem for the port, I trow!

But iron-rust and alum-spray
And chafing gear, and sun and dew
Vexed this lad and lassie gay,
Tears in their eyes, salt tears nor few;
And the hug relaxed with the failing glue.

But came in end a dismal night,
With creaking beams and ribs that groan,
A black lee-shore and waters white:
Dropped on the reef, the pair lie prone:
O, the breakers dance, but the winds they
moan!


## THE GOOD CRAFT SNOW BIRD

Strenuous need that head-wind be
From purposed voyage that drives at last
The ship, sharp-braced and dogged still,
Beating up against the blast.

Brigs that figs for market gather,
Homeward-bound upon the stretch,

Encounter oft this uglier weather
Yet in end their port they fetch.

Mark yon craft from sunny Smyrna
Glazed with ice in Boston Bay;
Out they toss the fig-drums cheerly,
Livelier for the frosty ray.

What if sleet off-shore assailed her,
What though ice yet plate her yards;
In wintry port not less she renders
Summer's gift with warm regards!

And, look, the underwriters' man,
Timely, when the stevedore's done,
Puts on his specs to pry and scan,
And sets her down, A, No. 1.

Bravo, master! Bravo, brig!
For slanting snows out of the West
Never the Snow-Bird cares one fig;
And foul winds steady her, though a pest.


## OLD COUNSEL
Of The Young Master of a Wrecked California Clipper

Come out of the Golden Gate,
Go round the Horn with streamers,
Carry royals early and late;
But, brother, be not over-elate
All hands save ship! has startled dreamers.


## THE TUFT OF KELP

All dripping in tangles green,
Cast up by a lonely sea
If purer for that, O Weed,
Bitterer, too, are ye?


## THE MALDIVE SHARK

About the Shark, phlegmatical one,
Pale sot of the Maldive sea,
The sleek little pilot-fish, azure and slim,

How alert in attendance be.
From his saw-pit of mouth, from his charnel
of maw
They have nothing of harm to dread,
But liquidly glide on his ghastly flank
Or before his Gorgonian head:
Or lurk in the port of serrated teeth
In white triple tiers of glittering gates,
And there find a haven when peril's abroad,
An asylum in jaws of the Fates!
They are friends; and friendly they guide him
to prey,
Yet never partake of the treat
Eyes and brains to the dotard lethargic and
dull,
Pale ravener of horrible meat.


## TO NED

Where is the world we roved, Ned Bunn?
Hollows thereof lay rich in shade
By voyagers old inviolate thrown
Ere Paul Pry cruised with Pelf and Trade.
To us old lads some thoughts come home
Who roamed a world young lads no more shall
roam.

Nor less the satiate year impends
When, wearying of routine-resorts,
The pleasure-hunter shall break loose,
Ned, for our Pantheistic ports:
Marquesas and glenned isles that be
Authentic Edens in a Pagan sea.

The charm of scenes untried shall lure,
And, Ned, a legend urge the flight
The Typee-truants under stars
Unknown to Shakespere's Midsummer-
Night;
And man, if lost to Saturn's Age,
Yet feeling life no Syrian pilgrimage.

But, tell, shall he, the tourist, find
Our isles the same in violet-glow
Enamoring us what years and years
Ah, Ned, what years and years ago!

Well, Adam advances, smart in pace,
But scarce by violets that advance you trace.

But we, in anchor-watches calm,
The Indian Psyche's languor won,
And, musing, breathed primeval balm
From Edens ere yet overrun;
Marvelling mild if mortal twice,
Here and hereafter, touch a Paradise.


CROSSING THE TROPICS
From "The Saya-y-Manto."

While now the Pole Star sinks from sight
The Southern Cross it climbs the sky;
But losing thee, my love, my light,
O bride but for one bridal night,
The loss no rising joys supply.

Love, love, the Trade Winds urge abaft,
And thee, from thee, they steadfast waft.

By day the blue and silver sea
And chime of waters blandly fanned
Nor these, nor Gama's stars to me
May yield delight since still for thee
I long as Gama longed for land.

I yearn, I yearn, reverting turn,
My heart it streams in wake astern
When, cut by slanting sleet, we swoop
Where raves the world's inverted year,
If roses all your porch shall loop,
Not less your heart for me will droop
Doubling the world's last outpost drear.

O love, O love, these oceans vast:
Love, love, it is as death were past!


THE BERG
A Dream

I SAW a ship of martial build
(Her standards set, her brave apparel on)
Directed as by madness mere

Against a stolid iceberg steer,
Nor budge it, though the infatuate ship went
down.
The impact made huge ice-cubes fall
Sullen, in tons that crashed the deck;
But that one avalanche was all
No other movement save the foundering
wreck.

Along the spurs of ridges pale,
Not any slenderest shaft and frail,
A prism over glass, green gorges lone,
Toppled; nor lace of traceries fine,
Nor pendant drops in grot or mine
Were jarred, when the stunned ship went
down.
Nor sole the gulls in cloud that wheeled
Circling one snow-flanked peak afar,
But nearer fowl the floes that skimmed
And crystal beaches, felt no jar.
No thrill transmitted stirred the lock
Of jack-straw needle-ice at base;
Towers undermined by waves, the block
Atilt impending, kept their place.
Seals, dozing sleek on sliddery ledges
Slipt never, when by loftier edges
Through very inertia overthrown,
The impetuous ship in bafflement went down.
Hard Berg (methought), so cold, so vast,
With mortal damps self-overcast;
Exhaling still thy dankish breath
Adrift dissolving, bound for death;
Though lumpish thou, a lumbering one
A lumbering lubbard loitering slow,
Impingers rue thee and go down,
Sounding thy precipice below,
Nor stir the slimy slug that sprawls
Along thy dense stolidity of walls.

THE ENVIABLE ISLES
From "Rammon."

Through storms you reach them and from
storms are free.
Afar descried, the foremost drear in hue,
But, nearer, green; and, on the marge, the sea

Makes thunder low and mist of rainbowed
dew.

But, inland, where the sleep that folds the hills
A dreamier sleep, the trance of God, instills
On uplands hazed, in wandering airs
aswoon,
Slow-swaying palms salute love's cypress tree
Adown in vale where pebbly runlets croon
A song to lull all sorrow and all glee.

Sweet-fern and moss in many a glade are here.
Where, strewn in flocks, what cheek-flushed
myriads lie
Dimpling in dream, unconscious slumberers
mere,
While billows endless round the beaches die.


## PEBBLES

I
Though the Clerk of the Weather insist,
And lay down the weather-law,
Pintado and gannet they wist
That the winds blow whither they list
In tempest or flaw.

II
Old are the creeds, but stale the schools,
Revamped as the mode may veer,
But Orm from the schools to the beaches
strays
And, finding a Conch hoar with time, he
delays
And reverent lifts it to ear.
That Voice, pitched in far monotone,
Shall it swerve? shall it deviate ever?
The Seas have inspired it, and Truth
Truth, varying from sameness never.

III
In hollows of the liquid hills
Where the long Blue Ridges run,
The flattery of no echo thrills,
For echo the seas have none;
Nor aught that gives man back man's strain

The hope of his heart, the dream in his brain.

IV
On ocean where the embattled fleets repair,
Man, suffering inflictor, sails on sufferance
there.

V
Implacable I, the old Implacable Sea:
Implacable most when most I smile serene
Pleased, not appeased, by myriad wrecks in
me.

VI
Curled in the comb of yon billow Andean,
Is it the Dragon's heaven-challenging crest?
Elemental mad ramping of ravening waters
Yet Christ on the Mount, and the dove in
her nest!

VII
Healed of my hurt, I laud the inhuman Sea
Yea, bless the Angels Four that there convene;
For healed I am ever by their pitiless breath
Distilled in wholesome dew named rosmarine.


## Poems From Timoleon

### LINES TRACED UNDER AN IMAGE OF AMOR THREATENING

Fear me, virgin whosoever
Taking pride from love exempt,
Fear me, slighted. Never, never
Brave me, nor my fury tempt:
Downy wings, but wroth they beat
Tempest even in reason's seat.


### THE NIGHT MARCH

With banners furled and clarions mute,
An army passes in the night;
And beaming spears and helms salute
The dark with bright.

In silence deep the legions stream,
With open ranks, in order true;
Over boundless plains they stream and
Gleam
No chief in view!

Afar, in twinkling distance lost,
(So legends tell) he lonely wends
And back through all that shining host
His mandate sends.


## THE RAVAGED VILLA

In shards the sylvan vases lie,
Their links of dance undone,
And brambles wither by thy brim,
Choked fountain of the sun!
The spider in the laurel spins,
The weed exiles the flower:
And, flung to kiln, Apollo's bust
Makes lime for Mammon's tower.


## THE NEW ZEALOT TO THE SUN

Persian, you rise
Aflame from climes of sacrifice
Where adulators sue,
And prostrate man, with brow abased,
Adheres to rites whose tenor traced
All worship hitherto.

Arch type of sway,
Meetly your over-ruling ray
You fling from Asia's plain,
Whence flashed the javelins abroad
Of many a wild incursive horde
Led by some shepherd Cain.

Mid terrors dinned
Gods too came conquerors from your Ind,
The book of Brahma throve;
They came like to the scythed car,
Westward they rolled their empire far,
Of night their purple wove.

Chemist, you breed
In orient climes each sorcerous weed
That energizes dream
Transmitted, spread in myths and creeds,
Houris and hells, delirious screeds
And Calvin's last extreme.

What though your light
In time's first dawn compelled the flight
Of Chaos' startled clan,
Shall never all your darted spears
Disperse worse Anarchs, frauds and fears,
Sprung from these weeds to man?

But Science yet
An effluence ampler shall beget,
And power beyond your play
Shall quell the shades you fail to rout,
Yea, searching every secret out
Elucidate your ray.


## MONODY

To have known him, to have loved him
After loneness long;
And then to be estranged in life,
And neither in the wrong;
And now for death to set his seal
Ease me, a little ease, my song!

By wintry hills his hermit-mound
The sheeted snow-drifts drape,
And houseless there the snow-bird flits
Beneath the fir-trees' crape:
Glazed now with ice the cloistral vine
That hid the shyest grape.


## LONE FOUNTS

Though fast youth's glorious fable flies,
View not the world with worldling's eyes;
Nor turn with weather of the time.
Foreclose the coming of surprise:
Stand where Posterity shall stand;
Stand where the Ancients stood before,

And, dipping in lone founts thy hand,
Drink of the never-varying lore:
Wise once, and wise thence evermore.


## THE BENCH OF BOORS

In bed I muse on Tenier's boors,
Embrowned and beery losels all;
A wakeful brain
Elaborates pain:
Within low doors the slugs of boors
Laze and yawn and doze again.

In dreams they doze, the drowsy boors,
Their hazy hovel warm and small:
Thought's ampler bound
But chill is found:
Within low doors the basking boors
Snugly hug the ember-mound.

Sleepless, I see the slumberous boors
Their blurred eyes blink, their eyelids fall:
Thought's eager sight
Aches, overbright!
Within low doors the boozy boors
Cat-naps take in pipe-bowl light.


## ART

In placid hours well-pleased we dream
Of many a brave unbodied scheme.
But form to lend, pulsed life create,
What unlike things must meet and mate:
A flame to melt, a wind to freeze;
Sad patience, joyous energies;
Humility, yet pride and scorn;
Instinct and study; love and hate;
Audacity, reverence. These must mate,
And fuse with Jacob's mystic heart,
To wrestle with the angel, Art.


## THE ENTHUSIAST
"Though He slay me yet will I trust in Him."

Shall hearts that beat no base retreat
In youth's magnanimous years
Ignoble hold it, if discreet
When interest tames to fears;
Shall spirits that worship light
Perfidious deem its sacred glow,
Recant, and trudge where worldlings go,
Conform and own them right?

Shall Time with creeping influence cold
Unnerve and cow? the heart
Pine for the heartless ones enrolled
With palterers of the mart?
Shall faith abjure her skies,
Or pale probation blench her down
To shrink from Truth so still, so lone
Mid loud gregarious lies?

Each burning boat in Caesar's rear,
Flames, No return through me!
So put the torch to ties though dear,
If ties but tempters be.
Nor cringe if come the night:
Walk through the cloud to meet the pall,
Though light forsake thee, never fall
From fealty to light.


SHELLEY'S VISION

Wandering late by morning seas
When my heart with pain was low
Hate the censor pelted me
Deject I saw my shadow go.

In elf-caprice of bitter tone
I too would pelt the pelted one:
At my shadow I cast a stone.

When lo, upon that sun-lit ground
I saw the quivering phantom take
The likeness of St. Stephen crowned:
Then did self-reverence awake.


THE MARCHIONESS OF BRINVILLIERS

He toned the sprightly beam of morning
With twilight meek of tender eve,
Brightness interfused with softness,
Light and shade did weave:
And gave to candor equal place
With mystery starred in open skies;
And, floating all in sweetness, made
Her fathomless mild eyes.


## THE AGE OF THE ANTONINES

While faith forecasts millennial years
Spite Europe's embattled lines,
Back to the Past one glance be cast
The Age of the Antonines!
O summit of fate, O zenith of time
When a pagan gentleman reigned,
And the olive was nailed to the inn of the
world
Nor the peace of the just was feigned.
A halcyon Age, afar it shines,
Solstice of Man and the Antonines.

Hymns to the nations' friendly gods
Went up from the fellowly shrines,
No demagogue beat the pulpit-drum
In the Age of the Antonines!
The sting was not dreamed to be taken from
death,
No Paradise pledged or sought,
But they reasoned of fate at the flowing feast,
Nor stifled the fluent thought,
We sham, we shuffle while faith declines
They were frank in the Age of the Antonines.

Orders and ranks they kept degree,
Few felt how the parvenu pines,
No law-maker took the lawless one's fee
In the Age of the Antonines!
Under law made will the world reposed
And the ruler's right confessed,
For the heavens elected the Emperor then,
The foremost of men the best.
Ah, might we read in America's signs
The Age restored of the Antonines.

# HERBA SANTA

## I

After long wars when comes release
Not olive wands proclaiming peace
Can import dearer share
Than stems of Herba Santa hazed
In autumn's Indian air.
Of moods they breathe that care disarm,
They pledge us lenitive and calm.

## II

Shall code or creed a lure afford
To win all selves to Love's accord?
When Love ordained a supper divine
For the wide world of man,
What bickerings o'er his gracious wine!
Then strange new feuds began.

Effectual more in lowlier way,
Pacific Herb, thy sensuous plea
The bristling clans of Adam sway
At least to fellowship in thee!
Before thine altar tribal flags are furled,
Fain wouldst thou make one hearthstone of
the world.

## III

To scythe, to sceptre, pen and hod
Yea, sodden laborers dumb;
To brains overplied, to feet that plod,
In solace of the Truce of God
The Calumet has come!

## IV

Ah for the world ere Raleigh's find
Never that knew this suasive balm
That helps when Gilead's fails to heal,
Helps by an interserted charm.

Insinuous thou that through the nerve
Windest the soul, and so canst win
Some from repinings, some from sin,
The Church's aim thou dost subserve.

The ruffled fag fordone with care

And brooding, God would ease this pain:
Him soothest thou and smoothest down
Till some content return again.

Even ruffians feel thy influence breed
Saint Martin's summer in the mind,
They feel this last evangel plead,
As did the first, apart from creed,
Be peaceful, man, be kind!

V
Rejected once on higher plain,
O Love supreme, to come again
Can this be thine?
Again to come, and win us too
In likeness of a weed
That as a god didst vainly woo,
As man more vainly bleed?

VI
Forbear, my soul! and in thine Eastern
chamber
Rehearse the dream that brings the long
release:
Through jasmine sweet and talismanic amber
Inhaling Herba Santa in the passive Pipe
of Peace.


OFF CAPE COLONNA

Aloof they crown the foreland lone,
From aloft they loftier rise
Fair columns, in the aureole rolled
From sunned Greek seas and skies.
They wax, sublimed to fancy's view,
A god-like group against the blue.

Over much like gods! Serene they saw
The wolf-waves board the deck,
And headlong hull of Falconer,
And many a deadlier wreck.


THE APPARITION
The Parthenon uplifted on its rock first
challenging the view on the approach to Athens.

Abrupt the supernatural Cross,
Vivid in startled air,
Smote the Emperor Constantine
And turned his soul's allegiance there.

With other power appealing down,
Trophy of Adam's best!
If cynic minds you scarce convert,
You try them, shake them, or molest.

Diogenes, that honest heart,
Lived ere your date began;
Thee had he seen, he might have swerved
In mood nor barked so much at Man.

The Return of the Sire de Nesle.
A.D. 16

My towers at last! These rovings end,
Their thirst is slaked in larger dearth:
The yearning infinite recoils,
For terrible is earth.

Kaf thrusts his snouted crags through fog:
Araxes swells beyond his span,
And knowledge poured by pilgrimage
Overflows the banks of man.

But thou, my stay, thy lasting love
One lonely good, let this but be!
Weary to view the wide world's swarm,
But blest to fold but thee.


## SUPPLEMENT

Were I fastidiously anxious for the symmetry of this book, it would close
with the notes. But the times are such that patriotism, not free from
solicitude, urges a claim overriding all literary scruples.

It is more than a year since the memorable surrender, but events have
not yet rounded themselves into completion. Not justly can we complain

of this. There has been an upheaval affecting the basis of things; to altered circumstances complicated adaptations are to be made; there are difficulties great and novel. But is Reason still waiting for Passion to spend itself? We have sung of the soldiers and sailors, but who shall hymn the politicians?

In view of the infinite desirableness of Re-establishment, and considering that, so far as feeling is concerned, it depends not mainly on the temper in which the South regards the North, but rather conversely; one who never was a blind adherent feels constrained to submit some thoughts, counting on the indulgence of his countrymen.

And, first, it may be said that, if among the feelings and opinions growing immediately out of a great civil convulsion, there are any which time shall modify or do away, they are presumably those of a less temperate and charitable cast.

There seems no reason why patriotism and narrowness should go together, or why intellectual impartiality should be confounded with political trimming, or why serviceable truth should keep cloistered because not partisan. Yet the work of Reconstruction, if admitted to be feasible at all, demands little but common sense and Christian charity. Little but these? These are much.

Some of us are concerned because as yet the South shows no penitence. But what exactly do we mean by this? Since down to the close of the war she never confessed any for braving it, the only penitence now left her is that which springs solely from the sense of discomfiture; and since this evidently would be a contrition hypocritical, it would be unworthy in us to demand it. Certain it is that penitence, in the sense of voluntary humiliation, will never be displayed. Nor does this afford just ground for unreserved condemnation. It is enough, for all practical purposes, if the South have been taught by the terrors of civil war to feel that Secession, like Slavery, is against Destiny; that both now lie buried in one grave; that her fate is linked with ours; and that together we comprise the Nation.

The clouds of heroes who battled for the Union it is needless to eulogize here. But how of the soldiers on the other side? And when of a free community we name the soldiers, we thereby name the people. It was in subserviency to the slave-interest that Secession was plotted; but it was under the plea, plausibly urged, that certain inestimable rights guaranteed by the Constitution were directly menaced, that the people of the South were cajoled into revolution. Through the arts of the conspirators and the perversity of fortune, the most sensitive love of liberty was entrapped into the support of a war whose implied end was the erecting in our advanced century of an Anglo-American empire based upon the systematic degradation of man.

Spite this clinging reproach, however, signal military virtues and achievements have conferred upon the Confederate arms historic fame, and upon certain of the commanders a renown extending beyond the sea, a renown which we of the North could not suppress, even if we would. In personal character, also, not a few of the military leaders of the South enforce forbearance; the memory of others the North refrains from disparaging; and some, with more or less of reluctance, she can respect. Posterity, sympathizing with our convictions, but removed from our passions, may perhaps go farther here. If George IV could, out of the graceful instinct of a gentleman, raise an honourable monument in the great fane of Christendom over the remains of the enemy of his dynasty, Charles Edward, the invader of England and victor in the rout of Preston Pans, upon whose head the king's ancestor but one reign removed had set a price, is it probable that the granchildren of General Grant will pursue with rancor, or slur by sour neglect, the memory of Stonewall Jackson?

But the South herself is not wanting in recent histories and biographies which record the deeds of her chieftains, writings freely published at the North by loyal houses, widely read here, and with a deep though saddened interest. By students of the war such works are hailed as welcome accessories, and tending to the completeness of the record.

Supposing a happy issue out of present perplexities, then, in the generation next to come, Southerners there will be yielding allegiance to the Union, feeling all their interests bound up in it, and yet cherishing unrebuked that kind of feeling for the memory of the soldiers of the fallen Confederacy that Burns, Scott, and the Ettrick Shepherd felt for the memory of the gallant clansmen ruined through their fidelity to the Stuarts, a feeling whose passion was tempered by the poetry imbuing it, and which in no wise affected their loyalty to the Georges, and which, it may be added, indirectly contributed excellent things to literature. But, setting this view aside, dishonorable would it be in the South were she willing to abandon to shame the memory of brave men who with signal personal disinterestedness warred in her behalf, though from motives, as we believe, so deplorably astray.

Patriotism is not baseness, neither is it inhumanity. The mourners who this summer bear flowers to the mounds of the Virginian and Georgian dead are, in their domestic bereavement and proud affection, as sacred in the eye of Heaven as are those who go with similar offerings of tender grief and love into the cemeteries of our Northern martyrs. And yet, in one aspect, how needless to point the contrast.

Cherishing such sentiments, it will hardly occasion surprise that, in looking over the battle-pieces in the foregoing collection, I have been tempted to withdraw or modify some of them, fearful lest in presenting, though but dramatically and by way of poetic record, the passions and epithets of civil war, I might be contributing to a bitterness which every sensible American must wish at an end. So, too, with the emotion of victory as reproduced on some pages, and particularly toward the close. It should not be construed into an exultation misapplied—an exultation as ungenerous as unwise, and made to minister, however indirectly, to that kind of censoriousness too apt to be produced in certain natures by success after trying reverses. Zeal is not of necessity religion, neither is it always of the same essence with poetry or patriotism.

There are excesses which marked the conflict, most of which are perhaps inseparable from a civil strife so intense and prolonged, and involving warfare in some border countries new and imperfectly civilized. Barbarities also there were, for which the Southern people collectively can hardly be held responsible, though perpetrated by ruffians in their name. But surely other qualities, exalted ones, courage and fortitude matchless, were likewise displayed, and largely; and justly may these be held the characteristic traits, and not the former.

In this view, what Northern writer, however patriotic, but must revolt from acting on paper a part any way akin to that of the live dog to the dead lion; and yet it is right to rejoice for our triumphs, so far as it may justly imply an advance for our whole country and for humanity.

Let it be held no reproach to any one that he pleads for reasonable consideration for our late enemies, now stricken down and unavoidably debarred, for the time, from speaking through authorized agencies for themselves. Nothing has been urged here in the foolish hope of conciliating those men, few in number, we trust, who have resolved never to be reconciled to the Union. On such hearts everything is thrown away except it be religious commiseration, and the sincerest.

Yet let them call to mind that unhappy Secessionist, not a military man, who with impious alacrity fired the first shot of the Civil War at Sumter, and a little more than four years afterward fired the last one into his heart at Richmond.

Noble was the gesture into which patriotic passion surprised the people in a utilitarian time and country; yet the glory of the war falls short of its pathos, a pathos which now at last ought to disarm all animosity.

How many and earnest thoughts still rise, and how hard to repress them. We feel what past years have been, and years, unretarded years, shall come. May we all have moderation; may we all show candor. Though, perhaps, nothing could ultimately have averted the strife, and though to treat of human actions is to deal wholly with second causes, nevertheless, let us not cover up or try to extenuate what, humanly speaking, is the truth, namely, that those unfraternal denunciations, continued through years, and which at last inflamed to deeds that ended in bloodshed, were reciprocal; and that, had the preponderating strength and the prospect of its unlimited increase lain on the other side, on ours might have lain those actions which now in our late opponents we stigmatize under the name of Rebellion. As frankly let us own, what it would be unbecoming to parade were foreigners concerned, that our triumph was won not more by skill and bravery than by superior resources and crushing numbers; that it was a triumph, too, over a people for years politically misled by designing men, and also by some honestly-erring men, who from their position could not have been otherwise than broadly influential; a people who, though, indeed, they sought to perpetuate the curse of slavery, and even extend it, were not the authors of it, but (less fortunate, not less righteous than we), were the fated inheritors; a people who, having a like origin with ourselves, share essentially in whatever worthy qualities we may possess. No one can add to the lasting reproach which hopeless defeat has now cast upon Secession by withholding the recognition of these verities.

Surely we ought to take it to heart that that kind of pacification, based upon principles operating equally all over the land, which lovers of their country yearn for, and which our arms, though signally triumphant, did not bring about, and which lawmaking, however anxious, or energetic, or repressive, never by itself can achieve, may yet be largely aided by generosity of sentiment public and private. Some revisionary legislation and adaptive is indispensable; but with this should harmoniously work another kind of prudence, not unallied with entire magnanimity. Benevolence and policy, Christianity and Machiavelli, dissuade from penal severities toward the subdued. Abstinence here is as obligatory as considerate care for our unfortunate fellowmen late in bonds, and, if observed, would equally prove to be wise forecast. The great qualities of the South, those attested in the War, we can perilously alienate, or we may make them nationally available at need.

The blacks, in their infant pupilage to freedom, appeal to the sympathies of every humane mind. The paternal guardianship which for the interval government exercises over them was prompted equally by duty and benevolence. Yet such kindliness should not be allowed to exclude kindliness to communities who stand nearer to us in nature. For the future of the freed slaves we may well be concerned; but the future of the whole country, involving the future of the blacks, urges a paramount claim upon our anxiety. Effective benignity, like the Nile, is not narrow in its bounty, and true policy is always broad. To be sure, it is vain to seek to glide, with moulded words, over the difficulties of the situation. And for them who are neither partisans, nor enthusiasts, nor theorists, nor cynics, there are some doubts not readily to be solved. And there are fears. Why is not the cessation of war now at length attended with the settled calm of peace? Wherefore in a clear sky do we still turn our eyes toward the South as the Neapolitan, months after the eruption, turns his toward Vesuvius? Do we dread lest the repose may be deceptive? In the recent convulsion has the crater but shifted Let us revere that sacred uncertainty which forever impends over men and nations. Those of us who always abhorred slavery as an atheistical iniquity, gladly we join in the exulting chorus of humanity over its downfall. But we should remember that emancipation was accomplished not by deliberate legislation; only through agonized violence could so mighty a result be effected. In our natural solicitude to confirm the benefit of liberty to the blacks, let us forbear from measures of dubious constitutional rightfulness toward our white countrymen, measures of a nature to provoke, among other of the last evils, exterminating hatred of race toward race. In imagination let us place ourselves in the unprecedented position of the Southerners, their position as regards the millions of ignorant manumitted slaves in their midst, for whom some of us now claim the suffrage. Let us be Christians toward our fellow-whites, as well as philanthropists toward the blacks, our fellow-men. In all things, and toward all, we are enjoined to do as we would be done by. Nor should we forget that benevolent desires, after passing a certain point, can not undertake their own fulfillment without incurring the risk of evils beyond those sought to be remedied. Something may well be left to the graduated care of future legislation, and to heaven. In one point of view the co-existence of the two races in the South, whether the negro be bond or free, seems (even as it did to Abraham Lincoln) a grave evil. Emancipation has ridded the country of the reproach, but not wholly of the calamity. Especially in the present transition period for both races in the South, more or less of trouble may not unreasonably be anticipated; but let us not hereafter be too swift to charge the blame exclusively in any one quarter. With certain evils men must be more or less patient. Our institutions have a potent digestion, and may in time convert and assimilate to good all elements thrown in, however originally alien.

But, so far as immediate measures looking toward permanent Re-establishment are concerned, no consideration should tempt us to pervert the national victory into oppression for the vanquished. Should plausible promise of eventual good, or a deceptive or spurious sense of duty, lead us to essay this, count we must on serious consequences, not the least of which would be divisions among the Northern adherents of the Union. Assuredly, if any honest Catos there be who thus far have gone with us, no longer will they do so, but oppose us, and as resolutely as hitherto they have supported. But this path of thought leads toward those waters of bitterness from which one can only turn aside and be silent.

But supposing Re-establishment so far advanced that the Southern seats in Congress are occupied, and by men qualified in accordance with those cardinal principles of representative government which hitherto have prevailed in the land, what then? Why, the Congressmen elected by the people of the South will, represent the people of the South. This may seem a flat conclusion; but, in view of the last five years, may there not be latent significance in it? What will be the temper of those Southern members? and, confronted by them, what will be the mood of our own representatives? In private life true reconciliation seldom follows a violent quarrel; but, if subsequent intercourse be unavoidable, nice observances and mutual are indispensable to the prevention of a new rupture. Amity itself can only be maintained by reciprocal respect, and true friends are punctilious equals. On the floor of Congress North and South are to come together after a passionate duel, in which the South, though proving her valor, has been made to bite the dust. Upon differences in debate shall acrimonious recriminations be exchanged?

Shall censorious superiority assumed by one section provoke defiant self-assertion on the other? Shall Manassas and Chickamauga be retorted for Chattanooga and Richmond? Under the supposition that the full Congress will be composed of gentlemen, all this is impossible. Yet, if otherwise, it needs no prophet of Israel to foretell the end. The maintenance of Congressional decency in the future will rest mainly with the North. Rightly will more forbearance be required from the North than the South, for the North is victor.

But some there are who may deem these latter thoughts inapplicable, and for this reason: Since the test-oath operatively excludes from Congress all who in any way participated in Secession, therefore none but Southerners wholly in harmony with the North are eligible to seats. This is true for the time being. But the oath is alterable; and in the wonted fluctuations of parties not improbably it will undergo alteration, assuming such a form, perhaps, as not to bar the admission into the National Legislature of men who represent the populations lately in revolt. Such a result would involve no violation of the principles of democratic government. Not readily can one perceive how the political existence of the millions of late Secessionists can permanently be ignored by this Republic. The years of the war tried our devotion to the Union; the time of peace may test the sincerity of our faith in democracy.

In no spirit of opposition, not by way of challenge, is anything here thrown out. These thoughts are sincere ones; they seem natural, inevitable. Here and there they must have suggested themselves to many thoughtful patriots. And, if they be just thoughts, ere long they must have that weight with the public which already they have had with individuals.

For that heroic band, those children of the furnace who, in regions like Texas and Tennessee, maintained their fidelity through terrible trials, we of the North felt for them, and profoundly we honor them. Yet passionate sympathy, with resentments so close as to be almost domestic in their bitterness, would hardly in the present juncture tend to discreet legislation. Were the Unionists and Secessionists but as Guelphs and Ghibellines? If not, then far be it from a great nation now to act in the spirit that animated a triumphant town-faction in the Middle Ages. But crowding thoughts must at last be checked; and, in times like the present, one who desires to be impartially just in the expression of his views, moves as among sword-points presented on every side.

Let us pray that the terrible historic tragedy of our time may not have been enacted without instructing our whole beloved country through terror and pity; and may fulfillment verify in the end those expectations which kindle the bards of Progress and Humanity.

## Poems From Battle Pieces

### THE PORTENT
1859

Hanging from the beam,
Slowly swaying (such the law),
Gaunt the shadow on your green,
Shenandoah!
The cut is on the crown
(Lo, John Brown),
And the stabs shall heal no more.

Hidden in the cap
Is the anguish none can draw;
So your future veils its face,
Shenandoah!
But the streaming beard is shown
(Weird John Brown),
The meteor of the war.

### FROM THE CONFLICT OF CONVICTIONS
1860-1

The Ancient of Days forever is young,
Forever the scheme of Nature thrives;
I know a wind in purpose strong

It spins against the way it drives.
What if the gulfs their slimed foundations
bare?
So deep must the stones be hurled
Whereon the throes of ages rear
The final empire and the happier world.

Power unanointed may come
Dominion (unsought by the free)
And the Iron Dome,
Stronger for stress and strain,
Fling her huge shadow athwart the main;
But the Founders' dream shall flee.
Age after age has been,
(From man's changeless heart their way they
win);
And death be busy with all who strive
Death, with silent negative.

Yea and Nay
Each hath his say;
But God He keeps the middle way.
None was by
When He spread the sky;
Wisdom is vain, and prophecy.


THE MARCH INTO VIRGINIA
Ending in the First Manassas
July, 1861

Did all the lets and bars appear
To every just or larger end,
Whence should come the trust and cheer?
Youth must its ignorant impulse lend
Age finds place in the rear.
All wars are boyish, and are fought by boys,
The champions and enthusiasts of the state:
Turbid ardors and vain joys
Not barrenly abate
Stimulants to the power mature,
Preparatives of fate.

Who here forecasteth the event?
What heart but spurns at precedent
And warnings of the wise,
Contemned foreclosures of surprise?

The banners play, the bugles call,
The air is blue and prodigal.
No berrying party, pleasure-wooed,
No picnic party in the May,
Ever went less loth than they
Into that leafy neighborhood.
In Bacchic glee they file toward Fate,
Moloch's uninitiate;
Expectancy, and glad surmise
Of battle's unknown mysteries.
All they feel is this: 't is glory,
A rapture sharp, though transitory,
Yet lasting in belaureled story.
So they gayly go to fight,
Chatting left and laughing right.

But some who this blithe mood present,
As on in lightsome files they fare,
Shall die experienced ere three days are
spent
Perish, enlightened by the vollied glare;
Or shame survive, and, like to adamant,
The throe of Second Manassas share.


**BALL'S BLUFF**
A Reverie
October, 1861


One noonday, at my window in the town,
I saw a sight, saddest that eyes can see
Young soldiers marching lustily
Unto the wars,
With fifes, and flags in mottoed pageantry;
While all the porches, walks, and doors
Were rich with ladies cheering royally.

They moved like Juny morning on the wave,
Their hearts were fresh as clover in its prime
(It was the breezy summer time),
Life throbbed so strong,
How should they dream that Death in a rosy
clime
Would come to thin their shining throng?
Youth feels immortal, like the gods sublime.

Weeks passed; and at my window, leaving

bed,
By night I mused, of easeful sleep bereft,
On those 'brave boys (Ah War! thy theft);
Some marching feet
Found pause at last by cliffs Potomac cleft;
Wakeful I mused, while in the street
Far footfalls died away till none were left.


## THE STONE FLEET
An Old Sailor's Lament
December, 1861

I have a feeling for those ships,
Each worn and ancient one,
With great bluff bows, and broad in the beam:
Ay, it was unkindly done.
But so they serve the Obsolete
Even so, Stone Fleet!

You'll say I'm doting; do you think
I scudded round the Horn in one
The Tenedos, a glorious
Good old craft as ever run
Sunk (how all unmeet!)
With the Old Stone Fleet.

An India ship of fame was she,
Spices and shawls and fans she bore;
A whaler when the wrinkles came
Turned off! till, spent and poor,
Her bones were sold (escheat)!
Ah! Stone Fleet.

Four were erst patrician keels
(Names attest what families be),
The Kensington, and Richmond too,
Leonidas, and Lee:
But now they have their seat
With the Old Stone Fleet.

To scuttle them, a pirate deed
Sack them, and dismast;
They sunk so slow, they died so hard,
But gurgling dropped at last.
Their ghosts in gales repeat
Woe's us, Stone Fleet!

And all for naught. The waters pass
Currents will have their way;
Nature is nobody's ally; 'tis well;
The harbor is bettered, will stay.
A failure, and complete,
Was your Old Stone Fleet.


## THE TEMERAIRE

Supposed to have been suggested to an Englishman of the old order by
the fight of the Monitor and Merrimac

The gloomy hulls in armor grim,
Like clouds o'er moors have met,
And prove that oak, and iron, and man
Are tough in fibre yet.

But Splendors wane. The sea-fight yields
No front of old display;
The garniture, emblazonment,
And heraldry all decay.

Towering afar in parting light,
The fleets like Albion's forelands shine
The full-sailed fleets, the shrouded show
Of Ships-of-the-Line.

The fighting Temeraire,
Built of a thousand trees,
Lunging out her lightnings,
And beetling o'er the seas
O Ship, how brave and fair,
That fought so oft and well,

On open decks you manned the gun
Armorial.
What cheerings did you share,
Impulsive in the van,
When down upon leagued France and
Spain
We English ran
The freshet at your bowsprit
Like the foam upon the can.
Bickering, your colors
Licked up the Spanish air,
You flapped with flames of battle-flags

Your challenge, Temeraire!
The rear ones of our fleet
They yearned to share your place,
Still vying with the Victory
Throughout that earnest race
The Victory, whose Admiral,
With orders nobly won,
Shone in the globe of the battle glow
The angel in that sun.
Parallel in story,
Lo, the stately pair,
As late in grapple ranging,
The foe between them there
When four great hulls lay tiered,
And the fiery tempest cleared,
And your prizes twain appeared,
Temeraire!

But Trafalgar is over now,
The quarter-deck undone;
The carved and castled navies fire
Their evening-gun.
O, Titan Temeraire,
Your stern-lights fade away;
Your bulwarks to the years must yield,
And heart-of-oak decay.
A pigmy steam-tug tows you,
Gigantic, to the shore
Dismantled of your guns and spars,
And sweeping wings of war.
The rivets clinch the iron clads,
Men learn a deadlier lore;
But Fame has nailed your battle-flags
Your ghost it sails before:
O, the navies old and oaken,
O, the Temeraire no more!


A UTILITARIAN VIEW OF THE MONITOR'S FIGHT

Plain be the phrase, yet apt the verse,
More ponderous than nimble;
For since grimed War here laid aside
His Orient pomp, 'twould ill befit
Overmuch to ply
The rhyme's barbaric cymbal.

Hail to victory without the gaud
Of glory; zeal that needs no fans
Of banners; plain mechanic power
Plied cogently in War now placed
Where War belongs
Among the trades and artisans.

Yet this was battle, and intense
Beyond the strife of fleets heroic;
Deadlier, closer, calm 'mid storm;
No passion; all went on by crank,
Pivot, and screw,
And calculations of caloric.

Needless to dwell; the story's known.
The ringing of those plates on plates
Still ringeth round the world
The clangor of that blacksmiths' fray.
The anvil-din
Resounds this message from the Fates:

War shall yet be, and to the end;
But war-paint shows the streaks of weather;
War yet shall be, but warriors
Are now but operatives; War's made
Less grand than Peace,
And a singe runs through lace and feather.


MALVERN HILL
July, 1862

Ye elms that wave on Malvern Hill
In prime of morn and May,
Recall ye how McClellan's men
Here stood at bay?
While deep within yon forest dim
Our rigid comrades lay
Some with the cartridge in their mouth,
Others with fixed arms lifted South
Invoking so
The cypress glades? Ah wilds of woe!

The spires of Richmond, late beheld
Through rifts in musket-haze,
Were closed from view in clouds of dust
On leaf-walled ways,

Where streamed our wagons in caravan;
And the Seven Nights and Days
Of march and fast, retreat and fight,
Pinched our grimed faces to ghastly plight
Does the elm wood
Recall the haggard beards of blood?

The battle-smoked flag, with stars eclipsed,
We followed (it never fell!)
In silence husbanded our strength
Received their yell;
Till on this slope we patient turned
With cannon ordered well;
Reverse we proved was not defeat;
But ah, the sod what thousands meet!
Does Malvern Wood
Bethink itself, and muse and brood?
We elms of Malvern Hill
Remember everything;
But sap the twig will fill:
Wag the world how it will,
Leaves must be green in Spring.


STONEWALL JACKSON
Mortally wounded at Chancellorsville
May, 1863

THE Man who fiercest charged in fight,
Whose sword and prayer were long
Stonewall!
Even him who stoutly stood for Wrong,
How can we praise? Yet coming days
Shall not forget him with this song.

Dead is the Man whose Cause is dead,
Vainly he died and set his seal
Stonewall!
Earnest in error, as we feel;
True to the thing he deemed was due,
True as John Brown or steel.

Relentlessly he routed us;
But we relent, for he is low
Stonewall!
Justly his fame we outlaw; so
We drop a tear on the bold Virginian's bier,

Because no wreath we owe.


## THE HOUSE-TOP
July, 1863
A Night Piece

No sleep. The sultriness pervades the air
And binds the brain, a dense oppression, such
As tawny tigers feel in matted shades,
Vexing their blood and making apt for ravage.
Beneath the stars the roofy desert spreads
Vacant as Libya. All is hushed near by.
Yet fitfully from far breaks a mixed surf
Of muffled sound, the Atheist roar of riot.
Yonder, where parching Sirius set in drought,
Balefully glares red Arson, there, and
there.
The Town is taken by its rats, ship-rats
And rats of the wharves. All civil charms
And priestly spells which late held hearts in
Awe
Fear-bound, subjected to a better sway
Than sway of self; these like a dream dissolve,
And man rebounds whole aeons back in
nature.
Hail to the low dull rumble, dull and dead,
And ponderous drag that shakes the wall.
Wise Draco comes, deep in the midnight roll
Of black artillery; he comes, though late;
In code corroborating Calvin's creed
And cynic tyrannies of honest kings;
He comes, nor parlies; and the Town,
redeemed,
Gives thanks devout; nor, being thankful,
heeds
The grimy slur on the Republic's faith
implied,
Which holds that Man is naturally good,
And, more is Nature's Roman, never to be
scourged.


## CHATTANOOGA
November, 1863

A kindling impulse seized the host

Inspired by heaven's elastic air;
Their hearts outran their General's plan,
Though Grant commanded there
Grant, who without reserve can dare;
And, "Well, go on and do your will,"
He said, and measured the mountain then:
So master-riders fling the rein
But you must know your men.

On yester-morn in grayish mist,
Armies like ghosts on hills had fought,
And rolled from the cloud their thunders loud
The Cumberlands far had caught:
To-day the sunlit steeps are sought.
Grant stood on cliffs whence all was plain,
And smoked as one who feels no cares;
But mastered nervousness intense
Alone such calmness wears.

The summit-cannon plunge their flame
Sheer down the primal wall,
But up and up each linking troop
In stretching festoons crawl
Nor fire a shot. Such men appall
The foe, though brave. He, from the brink,
Looks far along the breadth of slope,
And sees two miles of dark dots creep,
And knows they mean the cope.

He sees them creep. Yet here and there
Half hid 'mid leafless groves they go;
As men who ply through traceries high
Of turreted marbles show
So dwindle these to eyes below.
But fronting shot and flanking shell
Sliver and rive the inwoven ways;
High tops of oaks and high hearts fall,
But never the climbing stays.

From right to left, from left to right
They roll the rallying cheer
Vie with each other, brother with brother,
Who shall the first appear
What color-bearer with colors clear
In sharp relief, like sky-drawn Grant,
Whose cigar must now be near the stump
While in solicitude his back

Heaps slowly to a hump.

Near and more near; till now the flags
Run like a catching flame;
And one flares highest, to peril nighest
He means to make a name:
Salvos! they give him his fame.
The staff is caught, and next the rush,
And then the leap where death has led;
Flag answered flag along the crest,
And swarms of rebels fled.

But some who gained the envied Alp,
And, eager, ardent, earnest there
Dropped into Death's wide-open arms,
Quelled on the wing like eagles struck in
Air
Forever they slumber young and fair,
The smile upon them as they died;
Their end attained, that end a height:
Life was to these a dream fulfilled,
And death a starry night.


## ON THE PHOTOGRAPH OF A CORPS COMMANDER

Ay, man is manly. Here you see
The warrior-carriage of the head,
And brave dilation of the frame;
And lighting all, the soul that led
In Spottsylvania's charge to victory,
Which justifies his fame.

A cheering picture. It is good
To look upon a Chief like this,
In whom the spirit moulds the form.
Here favoring Nature, oft remiss,
With eagle mien expressive has endued
A man to kindle strains that warm.

Trace back his lineage, and his sires,
Yeoman or noble, you shall find
Enrolled with men of Agincourt,
Heroes who shared great Harry's mind.
Down to us come the knightly Norman fires,
And front the Templars bore.

Nothing can lift the heart of man
Like manhood in a fellow-man.
The thought of heaven's great King afar
But humbles us, too weak to scan;
But manly greatness men can span,
And feel the bonds that draw.


THE SWAMP ANGEL

There is a coal-black Angel
With a thick Afric lip,
And he dwells (like the hunted and harried)
In a swamp where the green frogs dip.
But his face is against a City
Which is over a bay of the sea,
And he breathes with a breath that is
blastment,
And dooms by a far decree.

By night there is fear in the City,
Through the darkness a star soareth on;
There's a scream that screams up to the zenith,
Then the poise of a meteor lone
Lighting far the pale fright of the faces,
And downward the coming is seen;
Then the rush, and the burst, and the havoc,
And wails and shrieks between.

It comes like the thief in the gloaming;
It comes, and none may foretell
The place of the coming, the glaring;
They live in a sleepless spell
That wizens, and withers, and whitens;
It ages the young, and the bloom
Of the maiden is ashes of roses
The Swamp Angel broods in his gloom.

Swift is his messengers' going,
But slowly he saps their halls,
As if by delay deluding.
They move from their crumbling walls
Farther and farther away;
But the Angel sends after and after,
By night with the flame of his ray
By night with the voice of his screaming

Sends after them, stone by stone,
And farther walls fall, farther portals,
And weed follows weed through the Town.

Is this the proud City? the scorner
Which never would yield the ground?
Which mocked at the coal-black Angel?
The cup of despair goes round.
Vainly he calls upon Michael
(The white man's seraph was he,)
For Michael has fled from his tower
To the Angel over the sea.
Who weeps for the woeful City
Let him weep for our guilty kind;
Who joys at her wild despairing
Christ, the Forgiver, convert his mind.


## SHERIDAN AT CEDAR CREEK
October, 1864

Shoe the steed with silver
That bore him to the fray,
When he heard the guns at dawning
Miles away;
When he heard them calling, calling
Mount! nor stay:
Quick, or all is lost;
They've surprised and stormed the post,
They push your routed host
Gallop! retrieve the day.

House the horse in ermine
For the foam-flake blew
White through the red October;
He thundered into view;
They cheered him in the looming.
Horseman and horse they knew.
The turn of the tide began,
The rally of bugles ran,
He swung his hat in the van;
The electric hoof-spark flew.

Wreathe the steed and lead him
For the charge he led
Touched and turned the cypress
Into amaranths for the head

Of Philip, king of riders,
Who raised them from the dead.
The camp (at dawning lost),
By eve, recovered, forced,
Rang with laughter of the host
At belated Early fled.

Shroud the horse in sable
For the mounds they heap!
There is firing in the Valley,
And yet no strife they keep;
It is the parting volley,
It is the pathos deep.
There is glory for the brave
Who lead, and nobly save,
But no knowledge in the grave
Where the nameless followers sleep.


IN THE PRISON PEN
1864

Listless he eyes the palisades
And sentries in the glare;
'Tis barren as a pelican-beach
But his world is ended there.

Nothing to do; and vacant hands
Bring on the idiot-pain;
He tries to think, to recollect,
But the blur is on his brain.

Around him swarm the plaining ghosts
Like those on Virgil's shore
A wilderness of faces dim,
And pale ones gashed and hoar.

A smiting sun. No shed, no tree;
He totters to his lair
A den that sick hands dug in earth
Ere famine wasted there,

Or, dropping in his place, he swoons,
Walled in by throngs that press,
Till forth from the throngs they bear
him dead

Dead in his meagreness.


## THE COLLEGE COLONEL

He rides at their head;
A crutch by his saddle just slants in view,
One slung arm is in splints, you see,
Yet he guides his strong steed, how
coldly too.

He brings his regiment home
Not as they filed two years before,
But a remnant half-tattered, and battered,
and worn,
Like castaway sailors, who, stunned
By the surf's loud roar,
Their mates dragged back and seen no
More
Again and again breast the surge,
And at last crawl, spent, to shore.

A still rigidity and pale
An Indian aloofness lones his brow;
He has lived a thousand years
Compressed in battle's pains and prayers,
Marches and watches slow.

There are welcoming shouts, and flags;
Old men off hat to the Boy,
Wreaths from gay balconies fall at his feet,
But to him, there comes alloy.

It is not that a leg is lost,
It is not that an arm is maimed,
It is not that the fever has racked
Self he has long disclaimed.

But all through the Seven Days' Fight,
And deep in the Wilderness grim,
And in the field-hospital tent,
And Petersburg crater, and dim
Lean brooding in Libby, there came
Ah heaven! what truth to him.


## THE MARTYR

Indicative of the passion of the people on the
15th of April, 1865

Goon Friday was the day
Of the prodigy and crime,
When they killed him in his pity,
When they killed him in his prime
Of clemency and calm
When with yearning he was filled
To redeem the evil-willed,
And, though conqueror, be kind;
But they killed him in his kindness,
In their madness and their blindness,
And they killed him from behind.

There is sobbing of the strong,
And a pall upon the land;
But the People in their weeping
Bare the iron hand;
Beware the People weeping
When they bare the iron hand.

He lieth in his blood
The father in his face;
They have killed him, the Forgiver
The Avenger takes his place,
The Avenger wisely stern,
Who in righteousness shall do
What the heavens call him to,
And the parricides remand;
For they killed him in his kindness,
In their madness and their blindness,
And his blood is on their hand.

There is sobbing of the strong,
And a pall upon the land;
But the People in their weeping
Bare the iron hand:
Beware the People weeping
When they bare the iron hand.


REBEL COLOR-BEARERS AT SHILOH
A plea against the vindictive cry raised by civilians shortly after the
surrender at Appomattox

The color-bearers facing death

White in the whirling sulphurous wreath,
Stand boldly out before the line;
Right and left their glances go,
Proud of each other, glorying in their show;
Their battle-flags about them blow,
And fold them as in flame divine:
Such living robes are only seen
Round martyrs burning on the green
And martyrs for the Wrong have been.

Perish their Cause! but mark the men
Mark the planted statues, then
Draw trigger on them if you can.

The leader of a patriot-band
Even so could view rebels who so could stand;
And this when peril pressed him sore,
Left aidless in the shivered front of war
Skulkers behind, defiant foes before,
And fighting with a broken brand.
The challenge in that courage rare
Courage defenseless, proudly bare
Never could tempt him; he could dare
Strike up the leveled rifle there.

Sunday at Shiloh, and the day
When Stonewall charged, McClellan's
crimson May,
And Chickamauga's wave of death,
And of the Wilderness the cypress wreath
All these have passed away.
The life in the veins of Treason lags,
Her daring color-bearers drop their flags,
And yield. Now shall we fire?
Can poor spite be?
Shall nobleness in victory less aspire
Than in reverse? Spare Spleen her ire,
And think how Grant met Lee.


AURORA BOREALIS
Commemorative of the Dissolution of armies at the Peace
May, 1865

What power disbands the Northern Lights
After their steely play?
The lonely watcher feels an awe

Of Nature's sway,
As when appearing,
He marked their flashed uprearing
In the cold gloom
Retreatings and advancings,
(Like dallyings of doom),
Transitions and enhancings,
And bloody ray.

The phantom-host has faded quite,
Splendor and Terror gone
Portent or promise and gives way
To pale, meek Dawn;
The coming, going,
Alike in wonder showing
Alike the God,
Decreeing and commanding
The million blades that glowed,
The muster and disbanding
Midnight and Morn.


## THE RELEASED REBEL PRISONER
June, 1865

Armies he's seen, the herds of war,
But never such swarms of men
As now in the Nineveh of the North
How mad the Rebellion then!

And yet but dimly he divines
The depth of that deceit,
And superstitution of vast pride
Humbled to such defeat.

Seductive shone the Chiefs in arms
His steel the nearest magnet drew;
Wreathed with its kind, the Gulf-weed drives
'Tis Nature's wrong they rue.

His face is hidden in his beard,
But his heart peers out at eye
And such a heart! like a mountain-pool
Where no man passes by.

He thinks of Hill, a brave soul gone;

And Ashby dead in pale disdain;
And Stuart with the Rupert-plume,
Whose blue eye never shall laugh again.

He hears the drum; he sees our boys
From his wasted fields return;
Ladies feast them on strawberries,
And even to kiss them yearn.

He marks them bronzed, in soldier-trim,
The rifle proudly borne;
They bear it for an heirloom home,
And he, disarmed, jail-worn.

Home, home, his heart is full of it;
But home he never shall see,
Even should he stand upon the spot:
'Tis gone! where his brothers be.

The cypress-moss from tree to tree
Hangs in his Southern land;
As weird, from thought to thought of his
Run memories hand in hand.

And so he lingers, lingers on
In the City of the Foe
His cousins and his countrymen
Who see him listless go.


"FORMERLY A SLAVE"
An idealized Portrait, by E. Vedder, in the Spring Exhibition of the National
Academy, 1865

The sufferance of her race is shown,
And retrospect of life,
Which now too late deliverance dawns upon;
Yet is she not at strife.

Her children's children they shall know
The good withheld from her;
And so her reverie takes prophetic cheer
In spirit she sees the stir.

Far down the depth of thousand years,
And marks the revel shine;
Her dusky face is lit with sober light,

Sibylline, yet benign.


## ON THE SLAIN COLLEGIANS

Youth is the time when hearts are large,
And stirring wars
Appeal to the spirit which appeals in turn
To the blade it draws.
If woman incite, and duty show
(Though made the mask of Cain),
Or whether it be Truth's sacred cause,
Who can aloof remain
That shares youth's ardor, uncooled by the
snow
Of wisdom or sordid gain?

The liberal arts and nurture sweet
Which give his gentleness to man
Train him to honor, lend him grace
Through bright examples meet
That culture which makes never wan
With underminings deep, but holds
The surface still, its fitting place,
And so gives sunniness to the face
And bravery to the heart; what troops
Of generous boys in happiness thus bred
Saturnians through life's Tempe led,
Went from the North and came from the
South,
With golden mottoes in the mouth,
To lie down midway on a bloody bed.

Woe for the homes of the North,
And woe for the seats of the South:
All who felt life's spring in prime,
And were swept by the wind of their place and
Time
All lavish hearts, on whichever side,
Of birth urbane or courage high,
Armed them for the stirring wars
Armed them, some to die.
Apollo-like in pride.
Each would slay his Python, caught
The maxims in his temple taught
Aflame with sympathies whose blaze
Perforce enwrapped him, social laws,

Friendship and kin, and by-gone days
Vows, kisses, every heart unmoors,
And launches into the seas of wars.
What could they else, North or South?
Each went forth with blessings given
By priests and mothers in the name of Heaven;
And honor in both was chief.
Warred one for Right, and one for Wrong?
So be it; but they both were young
Each grape to his cluster clung,
All their elegies are sung.
The anguish of maternal hearts
Must search for balm divine;
But well the striplings bore their fated parts
(The heavens all parts assign)
Never felt life's care or cloy.
Each bloomed and died an unabated Boy;
Nor dreamed what death was, thought it mere
Sliding into some vernal sphere.
They knew the joy, but leaped the grief,
Like plants that flower ere comes the leaf
Which storms lay low in kindly doom,
And kill them in their flush of bloom.


## AMERICA

I
Where the wings of a sunny Dome expand
I saw a Banner in gladsome air
Starry, like Berenice's Hair
Afloat in broadened bravery there;
With undulating long-drawn flow,
As tolled Brazilian billows go
Voluminously o'er the Line.
The Land reposed in peace below;
The children in their glee
Were folded to the exulting heart
Of young Maternity.

II
Later, and it streamed in fight
When tempest mingled with the fray,
And over the spear-point of the shaft
I saw the ambiguous lightning play.
Valor with Valor strove, and died:
Fierce was Despair, and cruel was Pride;

And the lorn Mother speechless stood,
Pale at the fury of her brood.

III
Yet later, and the silk did wind
Her fair cold form;
Little availed the shining shroud,
Though ruddy in hue, to cheer or warm.
A watcher looked upon her low, and said
She sleeps, but sleeps, she is not dead.
But in that sleeps contortion showed
The terror of the vision there
A silent vision unavowed,
Revealing earth's foundation bare,
And Gorgon in her hidden place.
It was a thing of fear to see
So foul a dream upon so fair a face,
And the dreamer lying in that starry shroud.

IV
But from the trance she sudden broke
The trance, or death into promoted life;
At her feet a shivered yoke,
And in her aspect turned to heaven
No trace of passion or of strife
A clear calm look. It spake of pain,
But such as purifies from stain
Sharp pangs that never come again
And triumph repressed by knowledge meet,
Power dedicate, and hope grown wise,
And youth matured for age's seat
Law on her brow and empire in her eyes.
So she, with graver air and lifted flag;
While the shadow, chased by light,
Fled along the far-drawn height,
And left her on the crag.


INSCRIPTION
For Graves at Pea Ridge, Arkansas

Let none misgive we died amiss
When here we strove in furious fight:
Furious it was; nathless was this
Better than tranquil plight,
And tame surrender of the Cause
Hallowed by hearts and by the laws.

We here who warred for Man and Right,
The choice of warring never laid with us.
There we were ruled by the traitor's choice.
Nor long we stood to trim and poise,
But marched and fell victorious!


## THE FORTITUDE OF THE NORTH
Under the Disaster of the Second Manassas

They take no shame for dark defeat
While prizing yet each victory won,
Who fight for the Right through all retreat,
Nor pause until their work is done.
The Cape-of-Storms is proof to every throe;
Vainly against that foreland beat
Wild winds aloft and wilder waves below:
The black cliffs gleam through rents in sleet
When the livid Antarctic storm-clouds glow.


## THE MOUND BY THE LAKE

The grass shall never forget this grave.
When homeward footing it in the sun
After the weary ride by rail,
The stripling soldiers passed her door,
Wounded perchance, or wan and pale,
She left her household work undone
Duly the wayside table spread,
With evergreens shaded, to regale
Each travel-spent and grateful one.
So warm her heart, childless, unwed,
Who like a mother comforted.


## ON THE SLAIN AT CHICKAMAUGA

Happy are they and charmed in life
Who through long wars arrive unscarred
At peace. To such the wreath be given,
If they unfalteringly have striven
In honor, as in limb, unmarred.
Let cheerful praise be rife,
And let them live their years at ease,
Musing on brothers who victorious died

Loved mates whose memory shall ever please.

And yet mischance is honorable too
Seeming defeat in conflict justified
Whose end to closing eyes is hid from view.
The will, that never can relent
The aim, survivor of the bafflement,
Make this memorial due.


AN UNINSCRIBED MONUMENT
On one of the Battle-fields of the Wilderness

Silence and solitude may hint
(Whose home is in yon piney wood)
What I, though tableted, could never tell
The din which here befell,
And striving of the multitude.
The iron cones and spheres of death
Set round me in their rust,
These, too, if just,
Shall speak with more than animated breath.
Thou who beholdest, if thy thought,
Not narrowed down to personal cheer,
Take in the import of the quiet here
The after-quiet, the calm full fraught;
Thou too wilt silent stand
Silent as I, and lonesome as the land.


ON THE GRAVE OF A YOUNG CAVALRY OFFICER KILLED IN THE
VALLEY OF VIRGINIA

Beauty and youth, with manners sweet, and
friends
Gold, yet a mind not unenriched had he
Whom here low violets veil from eyes.
But all these gifts transcended be:
His happier fortune in this mound you see.


A REQUIEM
For Soldiers lost in Ocean Transports

When, after storms that woodlands rue,
To valleys comes atoning dawn,
The robins blithe their orchard-sports renew;

And meadow-larks, no more withdrawn
Caroling fly in the languid blue;
The while, from many a hid recess,
Alert to partake the blessedness,
The pouring mites their airy dance pursue.
So, after ocean's ghastly gales,
When laughing light of hoyden morning
breaks,
Every finny hider wakes
From vaults profound swims up with
glittering scales;
Through the delightsome sea he sails,
With shoals of shining tiny things
Frolic on every wave that flings
Against the prow its showery spray;
All creatures joying in the morn,
Save them forever from joyance torn,
Whose bark was lost where now the
dolphins play;
Save them that by the fabled shore,
Down the pale stream are washed away,
Far to the reef of bones are borne;
And never revisits them the light,
Nor sight of long-sought land and pilot more;
Nor heed they now the lone bird's flight
Round the lone spar where mid-sea surges
pour.


## COMMEMORATIVE OF A NAVAL VICTORY

Sailors there are of the gentlest breed,
Yet strong, like every goodly thing;
The discipline of arms refines,
And the wave gives tempering.
The damasked blade its beam can fling;
It lends the last grave grace:
The hawk, the hound, and sworded nobleman
In Titian's picture for a king,
Are of hunter or warrior race.

In social halls a favored guest
In years that follow victory won,
How sweet to feel your festal fame
In woman's glance instinctive thrown:
Repose is yours, your deed is known,
It musks the amber wine;

It lives, and sheds a light from storied days
Rich as October sunsets brown,
Which make the barren place to shine.

But seldom the laurel wreath is seen
Unmixed with pensive pansies dark;
There's a light and a shadow on every man
Who at last attains his lifted mark
Nursing through night the ethereal spark.
Elate he never can be;
He feels that spirit which glad had hailed his
worth,
Sleep in oblivion. The shark
Glides white through the phosphorus sea.


A MEDITATION

How often in the years that close,
When truce had stilled the sieging gun,
The soldiers, mounting on their works,
With mutual curious glance have run
From face to face along the fronting show,
And kinsman spied, or friend, even in a foe.

What thoughts conflicting then were shared,
While sacred tenderness perforce
Welled from the heart and wet the eye;
And something of a strange remorse
Rebelled against the sanctioned sin of blood,
And Christian wars of natural brotherhood.

Then stirred the god within the breast
The witness that is man's at birth;
A deep misgiving undermined
Each plea and subterfuge of earth;
They felt in that rapt pause, with warning rife,
Horror and anguish for the civil strife.

Of North or South they reeked not then,
Warm passion cursed the cause of war:
Can Africa pay back this blood
Spilt on Potomac's shore?
Yet doubts, as pangs, were vain the strife
to stay,
And hands that fain had clasped again
could slay.

How frequent in the camp was seen
The herald from the hostile one,
A guest and frank companion there
When the proud formal talk was done;
The pipe of peace was smoked even 'mid the
war,
And fields in Mexico again fought o'er.

In Western battle long they lay
So near opposed in trench or pit,
That foeman unto foeman called
As men who screened in tavern sit:
"You bravely fight" each to the other said
"Toss us a biscuit!" o'er the wall it sped.

And pale on those same slopes, a boy
A stormer, bled in noon-day glare;
No aid the Blue-coats then could bring,
He cried to them who nearest were,
And out there came 'mid howling shot and shell
A daring foe who him befriended well.

Mark the great Captains on both sides,
The soldiers with the broad renown
They all were messmates on the Hudson's
marge,
Beneath one roof they laid them down;
And, free from hate in many an after pass,
Strove as in school-boy rivalry of the class.

A darker side there is; but doubt
In Nature's charity hovers there:
If men for new agreement yearn,
Then old upbraiding best forbear:
"The South's the sinner!" Well, so let it be;
But shall the North sin worse, and stand the
Pharisee?

O, now that brave men yield the sword,
Mine be the manful soldier-view;
By how much more they boldly warred,
By so much more is mercy due:
When Vicksburg fell, and the moody files
marched out,
Silent the victors stood, scorning to raise a
shout.

## Poems From Mardi

### WE FISH

We fish, we fish, we merrily swim,
We care not for friend nor for foe.
Our fins are stout,
Our tails are out,
As through the seas we go.

Fish, Fish, we are fish with red gills;
Naught disturbs us, our blood is at zero:
We are buoyant because of our bags,
Being many, each fish is a hero.
We care not what is it, this life
That we follow, this phantom unknown;
To swim, it's exceedingly pleasant,
So swim away, making a foam.
This strange looking thing by our side,
Not for safety, around it we flee:
Its shadow's so shady, that's all,
We only swim under its lee.
And as for the eels there above,
And as for the fowls of the air,
We care not for them nor their ways,
As we cheerily glide afar!

We fish, we fish, we merrily swim,
We care not for friend nor for foe:
Our fins are stout,
Our tails are out,
As through the seas we go.

### INVOCATION

Ha, ha, gods and kings; fill high, one and all;
Drink, drink! shout and drink! mad respond to
the call!
Fill fast, and fill full; 'gainst the goblet ne'er
sin;
Quaff there, at high tide, to the uttermost
rim:
Flood-tide, and soul-tide to the brim!

Who with wine in him fears? who thinks of his
cares?
Who sighs to be wise, when wine in him flares?
Water sinks down below, in currents full slow;
But wine mounts on high with its genial glow:
Welling up, till the brain overflow!

As the spheres, with a roll, some fiery of soul,
Others golden, with music, revolve round the
pole;
So let our cups, radiant with many hued wines,
Round and round in groups circle, our Zodiac's
Signs:
Round reeling, and ringing their chimes!

Then drink, gods and kings; wine merriment
brings;
It bounds through the veins; there, jubilant
sings.
Let it ebb, then, and flow; wine never grows
dim;
Drain down that bright tide at the foam beaded
rim:
Fill up, every cup, to the brim!


DIRGE

We drop our dead in the sea,
The bottomless, bottomless sea;
Each bubble a hollow sigh,
As it sinks forever and aye.

We drop our dead in the sea,
The dead reek not of aught;
We drop our dead in the sea,
The sea ne'er gives it a thought.

Sink, sink, oh corpse, still sink,
Far down in the bottomless sea,
Where the unknown forms do prowl,
Down, down in the bottomless sea.

'Tis night above, and night all round,
And night will it be with thee;
As thou sinkest, and sinkest for aye,

Deeper down in the bottomless sea.


## MARLENA

Far off in the sea is Marlena,
A land of shades and streams,
A land of many delights,
Dark and bold, thy shores, Marlena;
But green, and timorous, thy soft knolls,
Crouching behind the woodlands.
All shady thy hills; all gleaming thy springs,
Like eyes in the earth looking at you.
How charming thy haunts, Marlena!
Oh, the waters that flow through Onimoo;
Oh, the leaves that rustle through Ponoo:
Oh, the roses that blossom in Tarma.
Come, and see the valley of Vina:
How sweet, how sweet, the Isles from Hina:
'Tis aye afternoon of the full, full moon,
And ever the season of fruit,
And ever the hour of flowers,
And never the time of rains and gales,
All in and about Marlena.
Soft sigh the boughs in the stilly air,
Soft lap the beach the billows there;
And in the woods or by the streams,
You needs must nod in the Land of Dreams.


## PIPE SONG

Care is all stuff:
Puff! Puff!
To puff is enough:
Puff! Puff
More musky than snuff,
And warm is a puff:
Puff! Puff
Here we sit mid our puffs,
Like old lords in their ruffs,
Snug as bears in their muffs:
Puff! Puff
Then puff, puff, puff,
For care is all stuff,
Puffed off in a puff
Puff! Puff!

## SONG OF YOOMY

Departed the pride, and the glory of Mardi:
The vaunt of her isles sleeps deep in the sea,
That rolls o'er his corse with a hush,
His warriors bend over their spears,
His sisters gaze upward and mourn.
Weep, weep, for Adondo is dead!
The sun has gone down in a shower;
Buried in clouds the face of the moon;
Tears stand in the eyes of the starry skies,
And stand in the eyes of the flowers;
And streams of tears are the trickling brooks,
Coursing adown the mountains.
Departed the pride, and the glory of Mardi:
The vaunt of her isles sleeps deep in the sea.
Fast falls the small rain on its bosom that
sobs,
Not showers of rain, but the tears of Oro.


## GOLD

We rovers bold,
To the land of Gold,
Over the bowling billows are gliding:
Eager to toil,
For the golden spoil,
And every hardship biding.
See! See!
Before our prows' resistless dashes
The gold-fish fly in golden flashes!
'Neath a sun of gold,
We rovers bold,
On the golden land are gaining;
And every night,
We steer aright,
By golden stars unwaning!
All fires burn a golden glare:
No locks so bright as golden hair!
All orange groves have golden gushings;
All mornings dawn with golden flushings!
In a shower of gold, say fables old,
A maiden was won by the god of gold!

In golden goblets wine is beaming:
On golden couches kings are dreaming!
The Golden Rule dries many tears!
The Golden Number rules the spheres!
Gold, gold it is, that sways the nations:
Gold! gold! the center of all rotations!
On golden axles worlds are turning:
With phosphorescence seas are burning!
All fire-flies flame with golden gleamings!
Gold-hunters' hearts with golden dreamings!
With golden arrows kings are slain:
With gold we'll buy a freeman's name!
In toilsome trades, for scanty earnings,
At home we've slaved, with stifled yearnings:
No light! no hope! Oh, heavy woe!
When nights fled fast, and days dragged slow.
But joyful now, with eager eye,
Fast to the Promised Land we fly:
Where in deep mines,
The treasure shines;
Or down in beds of golden streams,
The gold-flakes glance in golden gleams!
How we long to sift,
That yellow drift!
Rivers! Rivers! cease your goings!
Sand-bars! rise, and stay the tide!
'Till we've gained the golden flowing;
And in the golden haven ride!


## THE LAND OF LOVE


Hail! voyagers, hail!
Whence e'er ye come, where'er ye rove,
No calmer strand,
No sweeter land,
Will e'er ye view, than the Land of Love!

Hail! voyagers, hail!
To these, our shores, soft gales invite:
The palm plumes wave,
The billows lave,
And hither point fix'd stars of light!

Hail! voyagers, hail!
Think not our groves wide brood with gloom;
In this, our isle,

Bright flowers smile:
Full urns, rose-heaped, these valleys bloom.

Hail! voyagers, hail!
Be not deceived; renounce vain things;
Ye may not find
A tranquil mind,
Though hence ye sail with swiftest wings.

Hail! voyagers, hail!
Time flies full fast; life soon is o'er;
And ye may mourn,
That hither borne,
Ye left behind our pleasant shore.


## Poems From Clarel

### DIRGE

Stay, Death, Not mine the Christus-wand
Wherewith to charge thee and command:
I plead. Most gently hold the hand
Of her thou leadest far away;
Fear thou to let her naked feet
Tread ashes, but let mosses sweet
Her footing tempt, where'er ye stray.
Shun Orcus; win the moonlit land
Belulled, the silent meadows lone,
Where never any leaf is blown
From lily-stem in Azrael's hand.
There, till her love rejoin her lowly
(Pensive, a shade, but all her own)
On honey feed her, wild and holy;
Or trance her with thy choicest charm.
And if, ere yet the lover's free,
Some added dusk thy rule decree
That shadow only let it be
Thrown in the moon-glade by the palm.


### EPILOGUE
If Luther's day expand to Darwin's year,
Shall that exclude the hope, foreclose the fear?

Unmoved by all the claims our times avow,

The ancient Sphinx still keeps the porch of
shade;
And comes Despair, whom not her calm may
cow,
And coldly on that adamantine brow
Scrawls undeterred his bitter pasquinade.
But Faith (who from the scrawl indignant
turns)
With blood warm oozing from her wounded
trust,
Inscribes even on her shards of broken urns
The sign o' the cross, the spirit above the dust!

Yea, ape and angel, strife and old debate
The harps of heaven and dreary gongs of hell;
Science the feud can only aggravate
No umpire she betwixt the chimes and knell:
The running battle of the star and clod
Shall run forever, if there be no God.

Degrees we know, unknown in days before;
The light is greater, hence the shadow more;
And tantalized and apprehensive Man
Appealing, Wherefore ripen us to pain?
Seems there the spokesman of dumb Nature's
train.

But through such strange illusions have they
passed
Who in life's pilgrimage have baffled striven
Even death may prove unreal at the last,
And stoics be astounded into heaven.

Then keep thy heart, though yet but
ill-resigned
Clarel, thy heart, the issues there but mind;
That like the crocus budding through the
snow
That like a swimmer rising from the deep
That like a burning secret which doth go
Even from the bosom that would hoard and
keep;
Emerge thou mayst from the last whelming
sea,
And prove that death but routs life into victory.

www.ingramcontent.com/pod-product-compliance
Lightning Source LLC
Chambersburg PA
CBHW070108070426

42448CB00038B/2216